CHICHARITO

CHICHARITO

THE JAVIER HERNANDEZ STORY

CHARLES SAMUEL

EBURY
PRESS

1 3 5 7 9 10 8 6 4 2

First published in 2012 by Ebury Press, an imprint of Ebury Publishing
A Random House Group company

The Random House Group Limited Reg. No. 954009

Addresses for companies within the Random House Group can be found at
www.randomhouse.co.uk

A CIP catalogue record for this book is available from the British Library

The Random House Group Limited supports The Forest Stewardship Council (FSC®), the
leading international forest certification organisation. Our books carrying the FSC label
are printed on FSC® certified paper. FSC is the only forest certification scheme endorsed by
the leading environmental organisations, including Greenpeace. Our paper procurement
policy can be found at www.randomhouse.co.uk/environment

MIX
Paper from
responsible sources
FSC® C023561

Designed by seagulls.net

Printed and bound in Great Britain by Butler Tanner & Dennis Ltd, Frome, Somerset

ISBN 9780091946821

To buy books by your favourite authors and register for offers visit
www.randomhouse.co.uk

CONTENTS

INTRODUCTION

Old Trafford, Manchester – 8 May 2011. Manchester United are about to entertain reigning champions Chelsea at home in a crucial league match.

The front cover of *United Review*, the official match programme, shows Javier 'Chicharito' Hernández scoring a dramatic late winner at home to Everton in the previous home league game. United's diminutive number 14 is smiling as he runs away from goal in a celebration which finishes with him lifting the team badge on his red shirt and putting a finger up to signal 'one' or 'first'. Only he knows.

United's first Mexican is still in his first season at Old Trafford, yet he's exceeded all expectations. He said himself that he expected to play only a few times as he settled at his new club and became accustomed to the physical demands of the Premier League. His manager Sir Alex Ferguson agreed, yet Hernández has become a firm fan favourite with a series of crucial – and usually late – finishes for United. When fans later look back at the highlights of the 2010–11 season, they number several Hernández goals as the high points. There was his vital winner at Valencia, his two goals at Stoke. Blackpool away, West Brom away, Marseille at home ... the list continues, as well it might, for he would score 20 goals. But today is Chelsea at home.

'I've talked to my team-mates about how to prepare for this part of the season,' he said a week ago. 'It's all about staying calm, focusing on the task in hand and believing in what you are doing.'

Most United fans believe in what he's doing but so – crucially – does his manager. Hernández has gone from starting most games on the bench to becoming United's first-choice striker alongside Wayne Rooney for the biggest games. And Chelsea at Old Trafford is as big as they come, especially as United have dropped league points against Arsenal in the previous game and Chelsea have enjoyed a late surge.

'Chelsea are a fine, experienced side, and I said months ago that they were the biggest threat to our championship hopes,' opines Ferguson.

Chelsea don't want to give up their title easily and they are feeling doubly vengeful against a United side who have knocked them out of the Champions League and prevented owner Roman Abramovich from realising his dream for another year.

Chelsea captain John Terry issues what the tabloid newspapers describe as a 'Battle Cry' when he claims that his side can beat United at Old Trafford and snatch the title. He has every reason to be confident. Chelsea have already beaten United at home in the league and they were the last team to beat United at Old Trafford over a year earlier, a win which all but sealed them the title.

The journalist who covers Chelsea for the *Ealing Gazette* thinks there will be a repeat of the victory a year earlier, while United fans interviewed for the programme pick out who they think United's key man will be. Six are interviewed and the names Rooney, Park, Valencia, Giggs, Ferdinand and Nani are mentioned, while Gary Neville singles out Ferdinand, Vidić and goalkeeper Edwin van der Sar, who is in the final month of an outstanding career.

Thirty seconds after kick-off, it becomes apparent just who United's man of the moment is when Chicharito receives a pass from Park, who in turn has got the ball from Giggs deep in the United half. These two incisive passes have split Chelsea in half. This is United at their attacking best and the Blues can't cope. Defender David Luiz, who had won rave reviews for his performance against United in an earlier league game, should have cut out the ball from Park. He didn't. Hernández is waiting and, after twitching his shoulder, wrong-foots Petr Čech and strikes the ball with his right foot into the net from 16 yards. It's the furthest that the Mexican has been from the goal-line for any of his United goals.

There are just 36 seconds on the clock and Old Trafford goes wild. Chelsea are devastated, United ecstatic as the stadium erupts like at no other time in the season – and Chicharito has provided many great moments to celebrate.

'It's all about staying calm, focusing on the task in hand and believing in what you are doing.'

United go on to win 2–1 and a record 19th title is within touching distance, with just one point needed from two games to play.

Few United fans had been inspired when the transfer activity was limited to just two relatively unknown and youthful acquisitions the previous summer. Chris Smalling had been a success, while Javier Hernández exceeded all expectations.

He was already a star in Mexico. After his performances and goals in the red of Manchester United, he quickly became one of the most popular footballers in the world. It was a dream come true for the intelligent and humble boy from Guadalajara, but it didn't happen overnight.

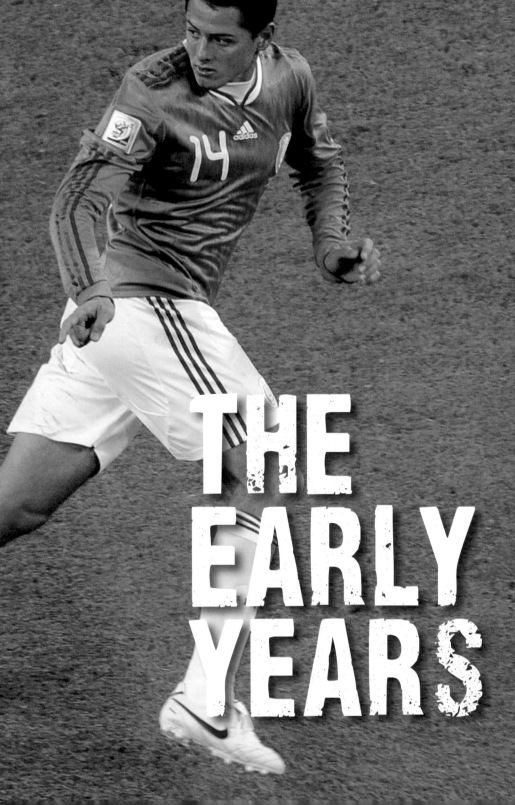

THE
EARLY
YEARS

the early years

Mexico can thank the British for taking football to the country in the late 19th century. British miners set up the country's first club, Pachuca Athletic Club, in 1900. Pachuca would play against clubs with similar anglicised names – Athletic, British Club, Reforma Rovers or Mexico City Cricket Club. All were based in or close to the capital Mexico City, where a considerable British community had grown up.

Mexico's second biggest city is Guadalajara, some 360 miles north-west of the capital. It formed its first club, Union FC, in 1906 and Union would later become Club Deportivo Guadalajara – the side Javier Hernández would play for.

Many of the British settlers left Mexico during the First World War and Mexican football became dominated by native Spanish speakers. The game became even more popular and attendances began to rise steadily. Four-, then five-figure crowds became the norm.

Of the current giants of Mexican football, Club America were founded in 1916, while Cruz Azul (Blue Cross in English) started life in 1927. Professional football was introduced in 1943. One game stood out above all: America v. Guadalajara – the so called 'El Superclásico', or the National Derby of Mexico. These were games between the biggest and most successful clubs; think Manchester United and Liverpool in England or Barcelona and Real Madrid in Spain.

Chicharito's grandfather Tomás Balcázar was born in Guadalajara in 1931 at a time when the city was undergoing rapid expansion, becoming an industrial powerhouse and one of the richest cities in Central America, not that Tomás was born into wealth.

'I was born very poor in the old Mexicaltzingo neighbourhood of Guadalajara,' he recalled. 'We're very humble people and I got everything I have now through football.

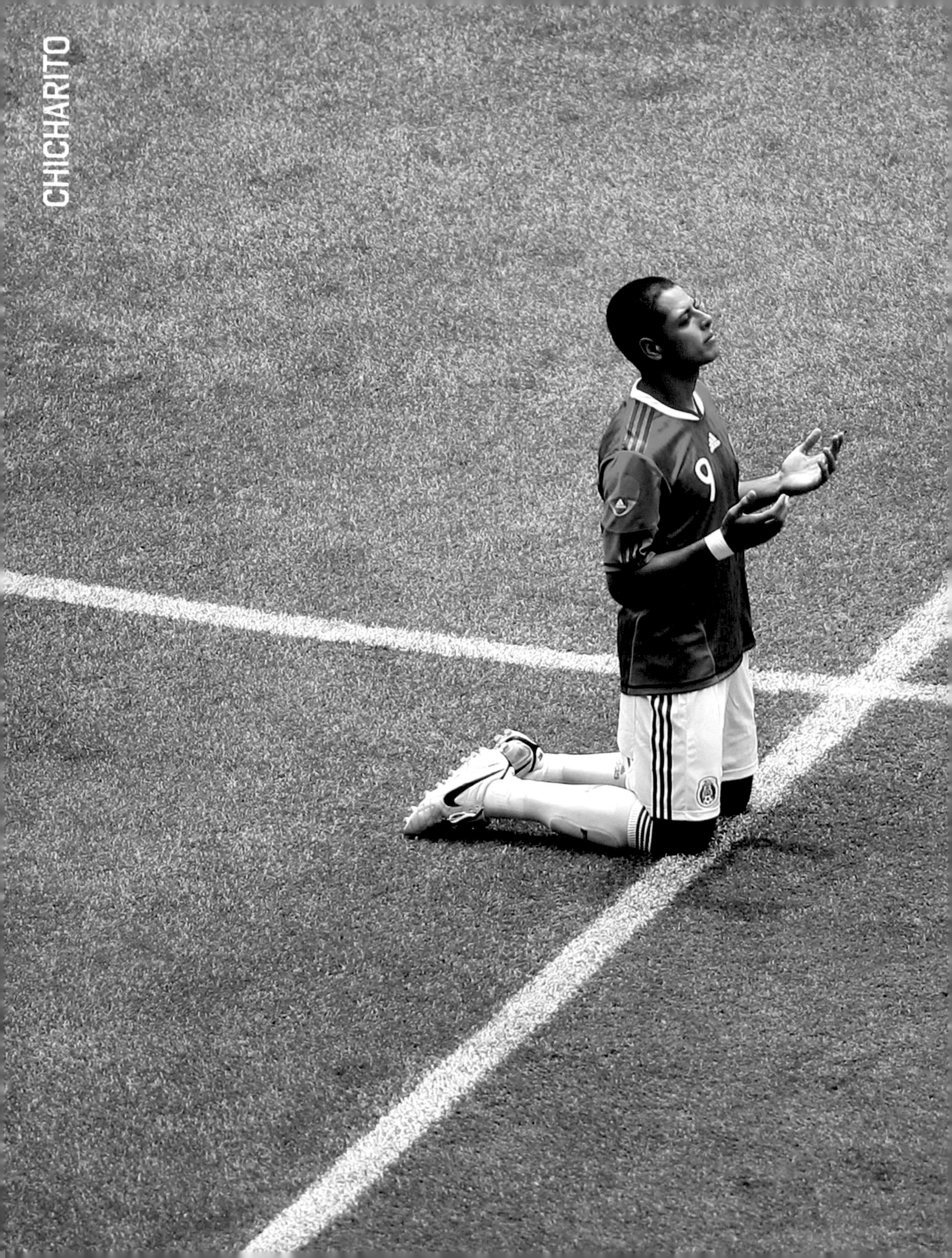
CHICHARITO

'I was born very poor in the old Mexicaltzingo neighbourhood of Guadalajara. We're very humble people and I got everything I have now through football.'

Tomás Balcázar

Playing enabled me to have things and later get married and then have six kids. All of them have professional titles.'

Known as 'Tommy' by fans, he was a striker who started out with amateur side Nacional of Guadalajara before joining Chivas – the nickname for Club Deportivo Guadalajara – where he played for a decade between 1948 and 1958. At the age of 22, he represented his country in the 1954 World Cup finals in Switzerland.

Tomás played in all four of Mexico's qualifying games against USA and Haiti home and away. Mexico registered four wins with 19 goals scored and just one conceded. Balcázar scored five and was in confident mood as Mexico crossed the Atlantic for the World Cup finals.

Sadly, Mexico lost both of their group games against seeded opponents. First they were hammered 5–0 by Brazil, then they lost 3–2 to France. The French had taken a two-goal lead, but Mexico clawed it back to 2–2, with Tomás scoring the equaliser in Geneva.

A last-minute France goal from the legendary Raymond Kopa gave France victory. Fifty-six years later, Balcázar's grandson would score for Mexico against France when he too was aged 22.

Tomás enjoyed the experience of travelling to Europe, but would fare much better for Chivas. He won the championship with them in 1957 (at the start of a run of seven championships in nine years for the team), and he was renowned for being an expert header of the ball. But Tomás Balcázar and his grandson wouldn't be the only people in their family to play for Mexico.

Mexico hosted two World Cups, in 1970 and 1986. The Azteca Stadium, which was used for both finals, boasted a capacity of 114,500 and was the biggest in the world. The 1986 tournament was where the term 'Mexican wave' was coined after the fans who stood up in a wave during the game.

Mexico's team in 1986 reached the quarter-final stage for only the second time in their history and they counted one Javier Hernández Gutiérrez among their squad. Unfortunately, El Chicharo – his green eyes earned him his nickname, which means 'Pea' in Mexican Spanish – who had the number 19 jersey, didn't play at all in Mexico's five-game run to the quarter-finals, before they went out on penalties to West Germany, but instead spent every minute on the bench.

Born in 1961 in Guadalajara, Javier Hernández Gutiérrez was a midfielder who enjoyed a fruitful professional career which spanned almost two decades, mainly for Club de Futbol Estudiantes – known by their nickname of 'Tecos' – who in 1994 went on to become Mexican champions.

Three big professional football teams play in the Guadalajara area: Chivas, Universidad de Guadalajara and Tecos, with Chivas easily the most popular. They can also boast more titles than any other Mexican side.

Although only 5 feet 6 inches, Hernández was a combative goal-scoring midfielder who is still in Tecos' top ten all-time leading goal-scorers.

In his private life, Chicharo met and married Silvia Balcázar, daughter of Tomás Balcázar and Lucha de Balcázar.

After 226 appearances and 46 goals in his eight years at the club, he left Tecos for Puebla FC in 1989, where he stayed for two seasons.

By that time Chicharo had become a father to Javier, who was born on 1 June 1988 in Guadalajara. His young family would move with him to Puebla, Mexico's fourth biggest city just east of Mexico City. Chicharo's new football team were about to enjoy a golden period in their history. With their new midfielder's help, Puebla won both the Mexican Cup and their second ever league title in 1990 – after beating Universidad de Guadalajara. It would be like Ryan Giggs joining Chelsea and helping them to the league and FA Cup at the expense of Manchester City.

Puebla and Universidad met in the two-legged final to decide the league. Hernández was among the scorers in the second-leg victory watched by a record crowd for football in Puebla of 60,000. The team became only the fourth in the history of Mexican football to win the league and cup double.

Chicharo was 29 and at his peak, but he did not play in the 1990 World Cup as El Tri – the popular name for the Mexican national side – were banned from entering all competitions for two years because of their use of over-age players in an Under-20 World Cup game. A Mexican junior team in a world championship qualifying tournament used four players who were over the age limit. The punishment meant that legendary Mexican players like Hugo Sánchez didn't play in Italia '90.

Puebla hit hard times themselves in the early 1990s, relegated due to irregularities, their club president prosecuted. Chicharo moved back to Tecos for a second spell and his growing family moved back to Guadalajara with him.

In 1995, Chicharo joined Club Atlético Morelia, the final club of his professional career. They were based 150 miles south-east of Guadalajara so it meant another move for the family. Morelia had been bought by a television company and wanted to become a major force in Mexican football. Chicharo did well and was recalled to the national team for two games, but he couldn't repeat the success he'd enjoyed at Puebla. He retired in 1998–99, the year of Manchester United's Treble, but he stayed in football in a series of coaching roles.

Chicharito has always listed his dad as his idol.

A STAR IS BORN

a star is born

The family's football hopes would now switch to Javier junior. He wouldn't disappoint, but his talent would take time to shine.

Javier started kicking a ball around at two or three but by the age of seven it wasn't clear that his family's footballing genes had been passed down.

'I never thought he would actually make it as a professional,' his father later said. 'We never thought he'd make the Mexican first division, but little by little he started maturing and at about age 15, we saw that change in him. When his goal was to become a professional footballer we supported him, but it was always up to him. Whatever he decided, we were there to help.'

'From being very small he was very restless,' recalled his grandfather. 'We used to go to our plot of land in front of the airport and we played little games of football. He used to play with us older folks and he used to slide-tackle us and take the ball. We saw he liked football because he was weaned on it since being in the cot.'

Javier had joined the youth ranks of Chivas at nine with Chivas Coras – a feeder team. He was a good pupil at school, though he once got in trouble for throwing a smoke bomb at a teacher, something he later admitted was the naughtiest thing he'd ever done.

Because he was the son of a former international, there was significant media interest in Javier. He'd yet to play a professional game, but explained that he 'had always been known as Chicharito – "the Little Pea" – because I was the son of my father'.

In an interview in May 2005 called 'Following Chicharo's example', a journalist asked Chicharito if he also played like his father. At that time, he operated as a right-winger and his answer was emphatic.

'I never thought he would actually make it as a professional … we supported him, but it was always up to him. Whatever he decided, we were there to help.'

Javier Hernandez, Sr.

'No, I have a very long way to go before I can be compared to him.' It showed his humility, but was also the correct answer. Chicharito has from the very beginning been careful and mature in interviews.

Most footballers talk about having had little interest in school because all they ever wanted to be was a footballer. They regret that, even if they make it, but Javier took a more balanced approach. He continued his studies in business administration classes at Universidad del Valle de Atemajac. He also lived at home and said in interviews that he counted on his family to keep his feet on the ground. He met his grandfather most days for lunch and even when he had become a star with Guadalajara said, 'I want people to treat me like the same guy. I want to enjoy the beautiful things – people recognising me in the street. But I don't want things to change a lot.'

When asked what he hoped to achieve in football, he replied: 'First and foremost, I want to play for the (Chivas) first team, win my place, then get called up to the national team. After that I can begin thinking about making the move to European football and to play in the World Cup finals like my dad and my grandad. Only then can I try to surpass what they achieved, which was certainly impressive.'

Chicharito did well and was set to play in the 2005 FIFA Under-17 World Championship in Peru – a tournament which Mexico won after beating Brazil 3–0 in the final – but injury ruled him out. He was getting used to football's highs and lows from an early age.

He made his Chivas debut at home to Necaxa the following year, 2006. Manchester United had played Necaxa in the World Club Championship in Rio six years before and were held to a draw. Back in the Mexican league, they would be beaten by the future United star who scored within five minutes of his debut in a 4–0 win.

Hernández came on for Omar Bravo, the long-standing Mexico international striker who would impress enough to win a move to Deportivo La Coruña in 2008. Told that he was coming on in the 82nd minute, he warmed up before praying to God on the touchline. Asked in one interview if he had a pre-match superstition or ritual, he replied: 'Before each game I get down on my knees and ask God to look after me and for things to go well.'

Five minutes later he scored his first goal in professional football. Describing the debut, he said: 'It was my first everything. My debut with the squad, my first time on the bench, my first game and my first goal.'

Of that goal, he said: 'I went straight to be with my dad and family after the game. They were crying with happiness. I didn't know what to do to celebrate but everyone was so happy.'

Chicharito has always cited the help from his family.

'The help he received from us is total, unequivocal,' said grandfather Tomás. 'When Chivas games ended normally we'd wait for him at the dressing room door and the first thing he'd ask is what we thought of his performance. Well, for us he's never played a perfect game! We'd say, "You played well but you lack a bit of this or that, and in that play where you chose to do this, you could've done something different." In other words, we always tried to help him improve because if you are telling him he's doing everything well, he won't improve. It's easy to say he was marvellous all the time.'

'After Chivas games sometimes he wouldn't get back on the bus with the team,' recalls his father. 'He liked to drive back with me and we would go through the game, go over the major incidents and talk it through.'

Chicharito made a further six appearances that season without scoring. Chivas won the Apertura title, but Chicharito was far from being a regular selection.

The Mexican season is divided into two separate tournaments, the Apertura, which runs from August to December, and the Clausura, which runs from January to June.

In the 2007–08 season Chicharito featured just five times for the first team, each time as a substitute. He played just 103 minutes of first-team football and didn't score. Three of those appearances came in the Copa Libertadores, the Champions League equivalent for South America. Even though Mexico is in Central America, their top clubs play in the Libertadores to boost the quality of the competition as they would be far better than any other teams in their own region.

Chicharito wasn't starved of football in 2007 though. That year, he represented Mexico in the Under-20 World Cup in Canada. His performances in Canada improved his stock further. It was also the first time that he came on to Manchester United's radar. There are always numerous scouts at the Under-20 World Cups, which are held every other year. The top talents are already signed to clubs, but if there's a real stand-out player on display, the top clubs will pay serious money for him.

'I went straight to be with my dad and family after the game. They were crying with happiness.'

At the previous Under-20 World Cup in the summer of 2005, Lionel Messi was easily the best player in the competition, the top scorer with six goals in seven games as Argentina triumphed. Messi's reserve-player contract with Barcelona, worth £100,000 a year, was upgraded to £3 million annually. He had shown that he was a stand-out among the best players of his age and that made Barça take even more notice of the prodigy in their ranks.

In 2007 in Canada, Chicharito's Mexico topped their group with three straight wins – the only one of the 24 finalists with a 100 per cent record. Hernández started the competition on the bench in Mexico's opening game against Gambia, but he soon made his mark after being introduced as a sub for Giovani dos Santos, then of Barcelona, in the 85th minute. Three minutes later he scored with a tap-in.

Chicharito was an unused sub in the next game, a 2–1 victory against Portugal, but the Mexico number 11 played 90 minutes in the final group stage win, a 2–1 win over New Zealand in Edmonton.

Mexico beat Congo 3–0 in the last 16, but Chicharito only came on in the last minute. He was by no means the first-choice striker and would play no more in the competition as he stayed on the bench while Mexico went out to eventual winners Argentina by a single goal in Ottawa in the quarter-finals. It was Argentina's toughest game of the competition and their outstanding player was Sergio Agüero, who won both the golden shoe for the top scorer with six goals and the golden ball for being the best player of the tournament. It was Argentina's fifth win in the past seven tournaments and with players like Agüero and Ángel di María, it wasn't a surprise.

A player who spent more time on the bench than on the field for the Under-20 team of a national side not ranked among the world's elite was no shoo-in to be a future Manchester United striker, but while Giovani dos Santos's flame flickered briefly at Barça, Hernández's time would come and he'd be far more impressive.

There was still a lot of uncertainty about his career. At the end of 2008, Hernández sat down with his parents and his agent Eduardo Hernández at a restaurant in Guadalajara. What was supposed to be a discussion about how to move his career forward turned into a counselling session. Tired of being kept on the bench, he wondered if heading back to college full-time might be a better career option than being a footballer. At 20, he would only be a few years older than the other students.

'He doubted himself; he doubted that he was capable of playing in the first division,' said his father, Javier Senior. 'As parents, we told him he had to be patient, but as a young player he was impatient. We talked to him about being persistent and in time everything would come.'

Recalling when he thought of quitting, Chicharito said: 'I didn't get many chances in the first team at Chivas, which led me to wonder "Is this the life I want for me?" I doubted if I was good enough to succeed as a footballer. I never saw myself working outside of football, but I had two tough years doubting if football was my destiny, or if God even wanted me to play football. I lost a lot of confidence and joy in that time, even in training.

'However I talked with my family, who told me to be patient, work hard and enjoy all that comes with being a footballer: not only to play games but to go to training, rest and work with the media, everything you have to endure in this profession.

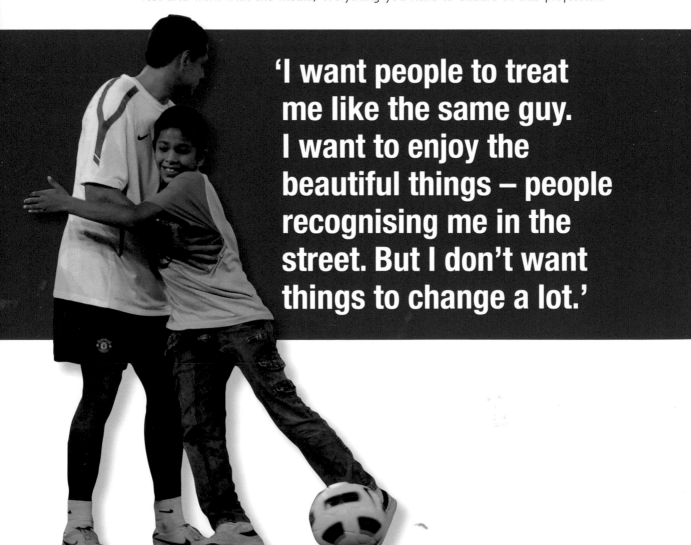

'I want people to treat me like the same guy. I want to enjoy the beautiful things – people recognising me in the street. But I don't want things to change a lot.'

When you are playing you must learn to accept the bad times as well as the good and enjoy the good. Trust is part of football.'

Chicharito's patience paid off. He became a regular for Chivas in the 2009 Apertura, when he scored 11 of Chivas' 23 goals in 17 games. His good form continued in the Libertadores. In one game against Everton of Chile in February 2009, he came off the bench in the 66th minute and scored twice.

He followed that up with eight more goals in nine games in the Clausura. Chicharito's versatility allowed him to adapt to play alongside Omar Arellano and Alberto Medina, his partners in the attack.

'They have given me a lot of confidence of late, I have enjoyed the continuity that every player needs at times to mature bit by bit, and I believe that is very important,' he said.

The media became more interested in the new striking sensation, but Chicharito dealt with this additional attention impressively. When one journalist asked him which striker he preferred to play alongside at Chivas, he could have been caught out by this simple question.

'I feel very comfortable playing alongside both of them,' he smiled. He was already a diplomat and he needed to be because his profile was getting bigger by the month and he was talking with more confidence.

Asked whether Chivas could win the Mexican Clausura 2009 and the Copa Libertadores, Chicharito replied: 'We can win both of them. Since the beginning of the season we have looked to qualify and become champions of both tournaments and thanks to God we have qualified in one.'

Chivas didn't win both but Chicharito's profile continued to rise. The media began to suggest that he should be selected for the Mexican national side.

He made his Mexico debut against Colombia on 30 September 2009. Describing the occasion, he said: 'It was the happiest day of my life when I was called up to the national team. I was very nervous, but it was an unforgettable experience to wear the colours of El Tri.'

His profile exploded in early 2010 – which is exactly when United started watching him closely. He scored seven goals in the opening four league games as Chivas headed the table with four straight wins.

Chicharito was in demand, but he was always down to earth in interviews, deflecting praise on to his team-mates. He claimed that he kept his feet on the ground: 'Thanks to all my team-mates, the coaching staff, to this whole great institution by which I am surrounded, and thanks to my family.'

Of his family he said that his grandfather Tomás was 'an example in life, as a person and as a football player'.

> **'It was the happiest day of my life when I was called up to the national team. I was very nervous, but it was an unforgettable experience.'**

He also explained in interviews that he loved his 'Chicharito' nickname, but that he was called 'Javi' at home. His family were his biggest motivation, his 'joy', his best quality. He listed water as his favourite drink, Abercrombie & Fitch as his favourite clothes label, his dog – a chow-chow – as his favourite pet and Katie Holmes as his favourite actress. He said that Germany was the country he most wanted to visit and that Seattle, New York and Cancún in Mexico were the best places he'd visited in his life so far. His favourite car was an FJ Toyota and his dream was twofold: to play in the World Cup finals and to play in Europe.

Hernández was asked his favourite European team and replied 'Juventus'. Asked which team he liked best out of Barcelona and Real Madrid, Chicharito replied 'Madrid'. And asked which stadium he would most like to play in he said Madrid's Santiago Bernabéu. Asked if he believed in God, Javi replied: 'Absolutely.'

Dutch giants PSV Eindhoven, the club which had nurtured the talents of Romário and later Jaap Stam and Ruud van Nistelrooy before selling the pair to United for a huge profit, were interested. More recently they had taken his team-mates Carlos Salcido and Francisco Rodríguez, both of whom had come through the Chivas youth system.

The Manchester United of 2000 would perhaps have waited for PSV to sign the player and watch his progress in Europe before making a huge bid. The new United wanted to cut out middle-men like PSV and secure the player at an earlier stage in his career.

Asked about a move to Europe, Chicharito said: 'I have always said that it is an aim for me, a dream I have, I hope to God that one day it will come true.'

In February 2010, he played against Bolivia in the first match of Mexico's 2010 preparation for the World Cup finals. He scored twice in the first 22 minutes and got an assist in a 5–0 win over Bolivia in San Francisco.

Hernández returned to the flock – another nickname for Chivas is El Rebaño Sagrado (The Sacred Flock) – where he continued to perform well and became the star attraction of his club, which also had the bonus of looking forward to moving into a spectacular new stadium in the summer of 2010.

'El Chicharito represents an example of perseverance, dedication and humility,' said die-hard Chivas fan Pablo López. 'He is an example to every player on the pitch.' But his days as a Chivas player were coming to an end.

'After a Chivas game my father gave me a business card from Manchester United,' smiled Chicharito. 'He said that this person wants to talk to you because they are interested in you. I saw the card and said, "I don't believe it".'

Manchester United? Chicharito thought his father was trying to fool him.

'Don't joke with me,' he said, then his father began to cry with happiness. At that, he realised his dad was serious.

'My father does not cry much,' added the striker. 'And I started to cry too. It was unbelievable. We had a lot of feelings in that moment. We wanted to scream, to be happy, to cry.'

The 'person' who had left the card was United's chief scout Jim Lawlor. Lawlor and Sir Alex Ferguson's brother Martin Ferguson travel extensively, watching emerging talent and United's upcoming opponents. One advantage is that they are not recognisable to most journalists and can operate in near secrecy.

Lawlor had been tipped off about Hernández by the former Mexican international footballer Marco Garcés. He'd spent four years studying for a sports science degree at Liverpool John Moores University and became friends with Lawlor, who worked at the university before joining United.

Garcés returned to Mexico to work for Pachuca's academy where Lawlor asked him to recommend Mexican players. (Pachuca are the Mexican team who played alongside United in the 2008 World Club Championship in Japan.) The name Javier Hernández came back in September 2009.

'I told him that he was excellent,' said Garcés, 'and that there was still room for improvement. I also said that he had all the attributes to do well in English football. Not only that, but that he was from a very good family with the right values. I also said that he already spoke English.'

Garcés later said that Hernández reminded him of the great Mexican striker Hugo Sánchez.

United sent a scout to watch Hernández in December 2009 and Lawlor himself visited Mexico for three weeks in February and March 2010 to make an in-depth assessment of the player.

Lawlor and Garcés watched several games in Mexico. They also travelled to Los Angeles, which boasts a huge Mexican population, to watch Mexico's 2–0 friendly win over fellow World Cup finalists New Zealand on 3 March 2010.

In the seemingly never-ending single-tiered stand of the Rose Bowl United saw their target come off the bench in the second half to score one goal and narrowly miss another in his first 10 minutes.

His goal was outstanding. Chicharito rose high above the New Zealand defence and hung in the air to meet a cross and head into the top-right corner. He ran away kissing the badge of Mexico, to the delight of the huge 90,526 crowd.

Arsenal's Carlos Vela also scored, but it was Chicharito's third goal in two international games after the 5-0 rout of Bolivia.

'He looked extremely hungry when he came on,' said New Zealand coach Ricki Herbert after the game. 'It will be an interesting proposition for the manager. He's an exciting player.'

Mexican football had found their latest star and because his maturity belied his 21 years, because he was articulate and telegenic, neither Chivas nor the Mexican Football Federation had any qualms about regularly putting him onstage at news conferences.

Everyone wanted to know about the Little Pea and journalists spoke to his family and former team-mates.

'We're very similar in the air,' said his proud grandad. 'He calculated exactly when to jump so that he wins the ball ahead of the defender. That's what I did.

'When I look at him I think I see the complete footballer. I don't see a prospect, I see a player who already has everything.'

The praise was flowing.

'You think, OK, here's this little midget,' added Chivas' USA forward Jesús Padilla, who played with Hernández for three years. 'But he's got some serious hops. He's amazing in the air.'

Asked if all this attention was too much, too soon, Nestor de la Torre, the director of Mexico's national teams, shook his head.

'We're talking about a player that is very down to earth, very simple,' de la Torre said. 'He's always been a player with the qualities on and off the field to be a Mexican soccer star.'

Chicharito returned to Chivas, where he was also the leading goal-scorer in Mexico at the time, notching up eight goals in seven games. Everybody wanted a piece of the Little Pea.

'A year ago, he didn't really exist for anybody,' said his agent Eduardo Hernández. 'Now, everybody wants him – sponsors, media, fans. He's got a very busy agenda.'

The pressure was on Mexico coach Javier Aguirre, a team-mate of Hernández's father in the 1986 World Cup finals, to make him a starter in the team which would play in the World Cup. At first Aguirre tried to play down the comments.

'The World Cup is in June,' he said. 'We're in March. We don't know who's going to make it. He is working just like everyone else. We have to go through a selection process and pick out the best.'

But then the coach was forced to concede that Hernández was 'going through a very good moment'. It was a nice problem for a manager.

Asked if he was looking forward to playing in South Africa, Chicharito said: 'I don't want to get ahead of myself, but at this point I have the same chances as everyone else. We'll just have to wait.'

Chicharito was still unheard of in Europe, but United had to make their move. Chief scout Jim Lawlor had seen more than enough to be convinced about his potential. He said as much to his boss, Sir Alex Ferguson.

'Jim filed a fantastic report on the boy, so last week we sent our club solicitor over there with Jim to do the deal,' said Ferguson. United would make their move for Javier Hernández before any of the other giants of world football stepped in.

'When you are playing you must learn to accept the bad times as well as the good and enjoy the good. Trust is part of football.'

SIGNING
FOR
UNITED

signing for united

Even Chicharito's agent didn't know that he was a target for Manchester United. The English club dealt directly with the Chivas president Rafael Lebrija and stressed the need for discretion. If negotiations could be kept under wraps United promised to send a team to play in a friendly to mark the opening of the new Chivas stadium in July 2010. Conveniently, United were already scheduled to be relatively nearby in Houston, Texas, a few days before in the final game of their North American pre-season tour.

United like to conclude transfers quietly. They feel that speculation can drive up the price of a player as agents or clubs invite other clubs to bid. Chief executive David Gill and Sir Alex Ferguson were delighted with the conduct of Chivas over the transfer – Chivas would get their friendly, without the $1 million match fee which United usually charge.

Alex Ferguson was, as usual, keeping a close eye on the process.

'I'd been watching him since October 2009 when he started to come into the Chivas team on a regular basis,' said the United manager. 'The amazing thing is that we managed to keep it so quiet.'

Since they had first spotted him playing for the Mexican Under-17 team five years earlier, United had kept an eye on Chicharito's progress. After his success in Chivas' first team, United became aware that the young prospect was starting to attract the attention of other giants of football.

The Reds had to make their move. Chicharito had never been a United fan, in fact he had not expressed any interest in joining an English team. He had always professed his desire to play in Europe, but had mentioned Juventus and the Bernabéu, rather than the English Premier League.

CHICHARITO

The Hernández family were equally tight-lipped. They even told Chicharito's grandfather Tomás Balcázar, who Javier speaks to every day, that they were travelling on a shopping trip to Atlanta in the United States.

Instead, they actually went to Manchester, Chicharito being accompanied by his dad and sister Ana Silvia, plus his agent.

'Ferguson wanted to meet with us so me and my family went to have lunch with him,' Chicharito said. 'I was very nervous, but very excited to meet the best coach in England. I know why he's been able to be so successful because he is just a really straightforward person.

'He's an extraordinary man – he makes such an impact on you and it is not just because of his accomplishments but because of the kind of person he is. We talked about football, he told us a few stories, you know, but otherwise we did not talk about much. He just wanted to meet my family and me and get to know us a bit.'

Alex Ferguson has a sure touch when courting prospective young signings. He knows the importance of face-to-face communication with the family and uses his considerable, surprising personal charm to good effect.

Chicharito successfully completed a medical and personal terms were agreed, not that it was made public.

'I got goose bumps when I realised I would be joining Manchester United,' he later said. 'These are the things you dream about. I longed for a move to Europe when I was a kid watching lots of football on TV.'

Hernández played his last game for Chivas on 27 March 2010, in which he scored in a 6–2 home win over Santos. Two weeks later, the travelling Mexicans then were guests of the club for United's 2010 Champions League quarter-final second leg against Bayern Munich.

'I got goose bumps when I realised I would be joining Manchester United.'

The first United fans knew of the signing was when the news broke on 8 April 2010. It was a good day for it to happen, for United had been knocked out of the Champions League the night before.

'I was at the game at Old Trafford and I think that the whole atmosphere, the way the fans express themselves, the way the country lives for football … it is very hard

to describe,' Chicharito said. 'I just wanted to jump on to the pitch and start playing. The support is amazing, whether the team is winning or losing, and the quality of the players and the league is well known.

'Football in England is more developed than it is in Mexico and the culture of the country means that the football is more about playing fair and honestly. Everyone is doing their best to make sure you get good football on the pitch. I like that.'

> **'The support is amazing, whether the team is winning or losing.'**

Following their defeat by the Bavarians, the United fans weren't feeling quite so enthusiastic. The mood around Old Trafford needed lightening and what better way than by announcing a new signing?

The initial reaction from Reds was: 'Who?' But opinions soon changed as fans quickly Googled the name of the 21-year-old Mexican and saw clips of the great goals he'd scored for Chivas.

One Mexican journalist told United fans:

'Hernández is the new superstar here. He's the highest scorer in the league the second half of this season, and has been one of the top Mexican scorers over the last couple of years. A product of the famous Chivas *cantera* (youth academy). Just broke into the national team, and has scored a couple of times in the friendlies this year already, and will definitely go to the World Cup.

'Good finisher, two-footed, very good in the air, intelligent player, not slow but not renowned for his pace. He looks a bit skinny but he's strong and if he builds up a bit, he should be able to adapt to the Premiership.'

It sounded promising.

Chicharito spoke about the transfer for the first time that day. A live broadcast was set up from Old Trafford to Mexico so a suited Chicharito could tell Chivas fans about the move and his five-year contract with United. His reaction was typically humble and generous.

'I'm happy and very grateful to the entire institution of Chivas,' he said. 'I feel much gratitude to everyone who has been with me and around me and I will remain the same person. I will not see myself as more nor less than anyone, I will remain the same guy from around here.

'I'm just full of gratitude to everyone who helped me accomplish this. Suddenly I'm going to be playing with the players I know from PlayStation and television. I'm living in a dream. I thank God that I am living it.'

It was during this interview that his grandfather found out that Chicharito had joined United.

'My daughter told me to watch the television,' said Tomás. 'And I saw that Javi was a member of Manchester.'

Then Chicharito did an interview for MUTV from an executive box in the Old Trafford main stand in which he spoke in good English and made all the right noises: 'All the impressions of the team and city (Manchester) are of happy things. I'm living a dream. Sir Alex Ferguson is a great person, maybe the best coach in the world.'

A few United fans bemoaned the signing because Hernández wasn't a big name. Others saw it as a sign of Fergie's commitment to buying emerging young talents following the January signing of Chris Smalling from Fulham. The likes of Ole Gunnar Solskjaer, Nani and Cristiano Ronaldo had all been relative unknowns when they signed for United. All went on to become club legends.

The transfer fee was not published and was listed as 'undisclosed', though it was widely reported to be £7 million, with the fee rising up to £10 million depending on the player's success. The transfer was also subject to Chicharito's application for a work permit being successful. All being well, he would become Manchester United's first ever Mexican player on 1 July 2010.

'I am delighted to reach agreement with Chivas to bring such an exciting young striker, who has been in such prolific form for both his club and his country,' Ferguson said. 'He will be a great addition to our squad and we look forward to welcoming our first Mexican player in the summer. We are equally excited to play our first game in Mexico, opening the magnificent new Chivas Stadium in July.'

United made a positive impression with Chicharito's dad too. Asked his opinion on meeting Ferguson, he said, 'It was amazing, incredible. For all the success he's had he seemed like a humble human being and it really grabbed my attention. It made an impression because I've met a lot of important people in different roles. But the gentleman has really got my respect. I never thought he'd be like he was: an exceptional man.'

Chicharito returned to Mexico, where he continued to study business administration at Universidad del Valle de Atemajac. His life had undergone a remarkable turnaround from less than 12 months earlier, when he'd considered a change of career after growing disillusioned with football – though he later admitted that his 'desperation' was his worst character trait.

The signing made sense. United had been accused of relying too much on Wayne Rooney – United's leading goal-scorer had come back from injury to play against Bayern Munich when he clearly was not close to being fit. There were other strikers like Dimitar Berbatov and Michael Owen, but no young prolific goal-scorers.

When asked about playing alongside Rooney, Chicharito said: 'I can already imagine that, but I want to go step by step because it is a dream to be here. And first I want to earn a place in the national team. I do not want to run yet. It's better to go step by step, and worry about other things as my career develops.'

Hernández may have wanted to take things slowly, but now he could anticipate the two fantastic prospects of taking part in the World Cup finals and playing for Manchester United in the English Premier League.

The reaction back home was positive. While the Chivas fans didn't want to lose their best player, they understood that he had a chance he couldn't refuse. Many promising Mexicans are talked of as being good enough to play in a major European league but few achieve the dream. Of those who do cross the Atlantic, only a handful play for big clubs. The highest profile Mexican in recent years was Rafa Márquez, the Mexican captain and Barcelona midfielder/defender. When he moved to New York in 2010 to team up with his former team-mate Thierry Henry, it meant that winger Andrés Guardado, who was playing with Deportivo La Coruña in Spain, was the highest profile Mexican abroad along with Tottenham's Giovani dos Santos.

The Chivas fans wished Chicharito well.

'He gave us the satisfaction of being our top scorer for two seasons,' said Rosa Covarrubias, a Chivas fan and sports journalist. 'He was good enough to be the focal point of the team for two seasons at such an early age.'

'CH14 (for that's what he was known as by many in Mexico) was a reference point, the standard bearer for the team in his short stay at the Flock,' added Juan Carlos Rubio Beltrán. 'He was undoubtedly the star man in our attack.'

And some Chivas fans remain hopeful that he'll return.

'We sowed the seed and watched you grow,' says Joaquín Miranda, 'but you were plucked to go to Europe. We will await, when the time comes, your return to where you belong ... The Sacred Flock. Go, Chicharito!'

THE 2010 WORLD CUP FINALS

the 2010 world cup finals

Expectations were huge in Mexico ahead of the 2010 World Cup finals in South Africa. Like in England, the media whips the football-obsessed population into a frenzy where they actually believe they have a chance of winning the tournament – despite every other indicator pointing towards the national team being a second-tier power on the international stage.

'Mexico is a football-crazy country and the people are very loyal to the national team,' said winger Andrés Guardado, the man who would be supplying the crosses for Chicharito.

'They know that we have a good team and expect us to represent them well. We are expected to qualify from our group. Mexico has done this in the last five World Cup finals. Once we get through, who knows? We'd hope to reach the quarter- or even semi-finals.'

Asked to point out the most promising talents, Guardado smiled and said, 'We have players breaking through like Javier Hernández. I think we might surprise some people.'

Since playing his final game for Chivas in late March 2010, Chicharito had signed for United. His last games for Mexico had been in March when he scored in a 2–1 win over North Korea and featured in a disappointing 0–0 draw with Iceland.

However, Chicharito hadn't played any games in April and his competitive matches had been limited to games for Mexico. United didn't want their new signing to be injured playing for Chivas, but they were happy to let him play for his country. Very happy, in fact, because United were still waiting on a work permit which had been held up because he had played in less than 75 per cent of Mexico's internationals in the previous two years. Now, he would become a regular.

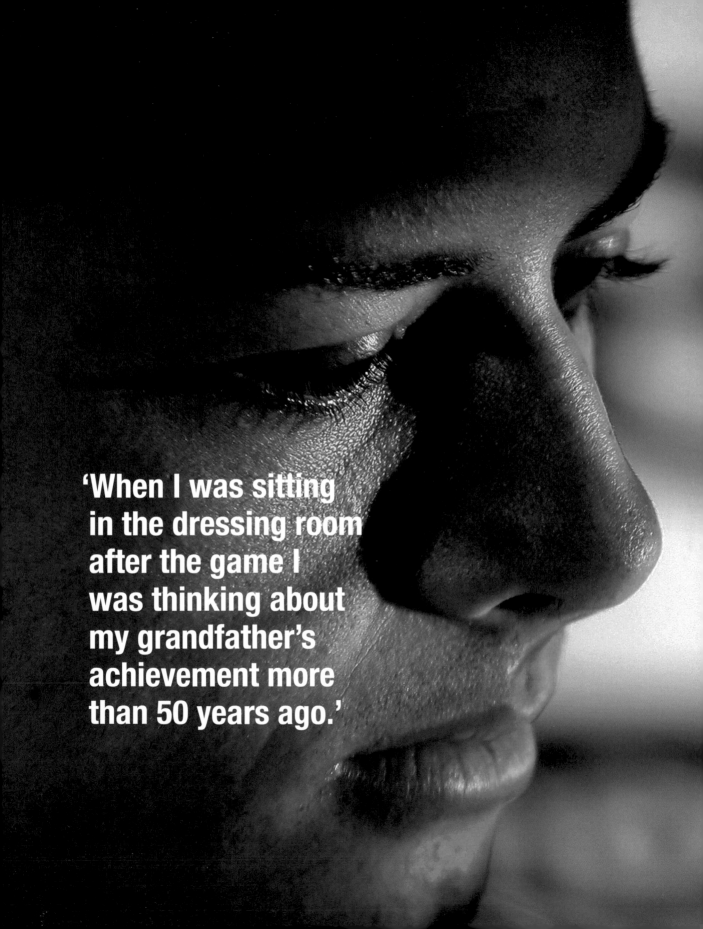

'When I was sitting in the dressing room after the game I was thinking about my grandfather's achievement more than 50 years ago.'

'We have players breaking through like Javier Hernández. I think we might surprise some people.'
Andrés Guardado

Chicharito started in a series of friendlies against Ecuador, Senegal, Angola and Chile in May 2010.

He didn't impress in the 0–0 draw against Ecuador in New York and missed an easy chance in the seventh minute. Mexicans put the poor performance down to the fact that they were missing most of their European-based players, but they beat Senegal three days later. Hernández came close, but didn't score. He started on the bench in his third friendly in a week in a 1–0 win against Angola in Houston's Reliant stadium. Hernández played the last 15 minutes without scoring, with the media praising Mexico's fourth consecutive clean sheet rather than their attack.

Mexico's final home friendly before the World Cup was played in front of over 93,000 at the Azteca Stadium and brought an impressive 1–0 win against fellow World Cup finalists Chile. Hernández started, but missed several chances to score. He sent one ball flying over the empty net in the first half before beating two defenders only to hit the post with his shot. This was becoming a pattern as he found his international feet. Still, Mexico won and kept another clean sheet against a team rated very highly in South America.

Their next stop on the way to South Africa was Wembley Stadium for a friendly with England. This was the first chance for most Manchester United fans to see their new signing play. With Mexico 2–1 down, Chicharito came off the bench at half-time. Within two minutes the Mexicans had conceded another goal but the scoreline hid the fact that Mexico were the better team for large parts of the game. Hernández didn't see much of the ball but showed glimpses of his talent as he was well marshalled by Jamie Carragher and Ledley King.

On 27 May, Sir Alex Ferguson attended a hearing with the British authorities and explained why he felt Hernández should be granted a work permit. His arguments were successful. United had formally signed a Mexican for the first time.

The night before the hearing, Hernández featured in a 2–1 defeat to a Holland team who would go on to reach the World Cup final. He scored with a decisive downward header from six yards out in the 74th minute after a looping cross over the Dutch defenders from Jorge Torres. The headlines, however, were grabbed by the star of the match Robin van Persie, who got both Holland goals in front of 22,000 in Freiburg.

Hernández was getting warmed up in Mexico's German training camp and scored twice in a 5–1 win against Gambia on 30 May. The goals were starting to flow as his international experience increased.

On 3 June, Mexico played – and beat – reigning world champions Italy 2–1 in their last friendly before the tournament. That Chicharito started that game looked promising for his World Cup prospects, but disappointment would follow as he

CHICHARITO

warmed the bench in South Africa for Mexico's first game – the opening match of the 2010 World Cup against the host nation South Africa in Soweto, Johannesburg.

A global TV audience of over 500 million saw Mexico, ranked 17th in the world, fall behind to a stunning goal from South Africa, ranked 83rd. The game was seen as a huge success, with the football and new stadium praised, but Mexico were trailing when Hernández was finally introduced in the 70th minute. He'd matched his grandfather and eclipsed his father by playing in the World Cup finals.

Nine minutes later Mexico were level after a Rafa Márquez goal. The night belonged to South Africa, but El Tri were satisfied with their draw in such an emotional hothouse.

Hernández could count on the support of his family in South Africa as his father had stepped down from his job as Chivas' reserve team manager after taking the decision to follow his son to the finals.

The family travelled to Polokwane for Mexico's next game, a key match against France, the 2006 finalists. Mexico hadn't beaten France in six previous attempts and Hernández didn't start, but came on to the field after 55 minutes with the score at 0–0. Nine minutes later, Chicharito sprang the offside trap to race on to Rafael Márquez's pass. There was still a lot for him to do, but he rounded goalkeeper Hugo Lloris and slotted the ball home with confidence. He'd emulated his grandfather, who had scored against France in the 1954 World Cup. Another Mexico substitute, Blanco, made it two.

Chicharito could not hide his joy. 'I am so proud to have scored this goal and when I was sitting in the dressing room after the game I was thinking about my grandfather's achievement more than 50 years ago,' he beamed after the game.

'I have not spoken to him or any other members of my family yet but I know they will all be very happy. I am very happy to be joining Manchester United and am looking forward to moving there soon. But right now I am thinking 100 per cent about Mexico and the World Cup, of beating Uruguay in our next game and going as far as we can in this competition.'

Chicharito's family have always been close to his heart. In one interview in South Africa, he was asked to describe what type of person he was away from the pitch. 'Happy, homely and laid-back,' was his reply. In the same interview he said that his favourite other sport was tennis, that Mexico had the most beautiful women in the world and that the last book he read was Thierry Henry's biography. He listed his favourite food as a banana, said that his greatest fear was failure and that 'unpunctuality' made him angry.

The French players were angry for reasons other than losing to the unfancied Mexicans. Their squad would go into meltdown after a players' revolt, with United's Patrice Evra at the core of the unhappy players.

Mexico next faced a Uruguay side with a former United striker, Diego Forlán, as their talisman, in the final group game.

Everyone predicted a draw that would have been good enough for both sides to progress at the expense of France and South Africa. It didn't happen and that wasn't the only surprise – Mexican fans were stunned when Hernández started on the bench as the veteran Cuauhtémoc Blanco, 37, was preferred. Hernández understood – he'd described Blanco as the best Mexican player several times.

Luis Suárez scored the only goal of the game and Chicharito came off the bench in the 62nd minute to try and equalise. He couldn't, but Mexico still went through to the last 16. Finishing second wasn't good news for their prospects – they would face Diego Maradona's Argentina in a re-run of one of the best games of the 2006 World Cup finals in Germany.

Hernández started in the biggest game of his career to date in front of 84,377 in Soweto's Soccer City. He was up against Lionel Messi, Javier Mascherano, Ángel di María, Carlos Tévez, Juan Sebastián Verón and Gabriel Heinze. This was the big time.

Argentina were favourites to advance but Mexico were the better team in the opening encounters. Carlos Salcido's 30-yard shot came off the bar and Guardado shot wide, but it was Maradona's side which took the lead after 25 minutes through a goal which should never have been. Messi threaded a ball to Tévez, who was in an offside position when he headed the ball in. The Mexicans were right to be outraged and protested right up to half-time. They were absolutely fuming and maybe this knocked their concentration because they never recovered from the awful officiating and fell further behind when Gonzalo Higuaín added a second on 33 minutes.

Tévez made it 3–0 seven minutes after the break before Chicharito got a consolation goal after 71 minutes. He turned beautifully to lose Martín Demichelis before burying a shot past Sergio Romero. How United could have done with him a few months earlier when Rooney was rushed back to play against Bayern Munich and their paceless defender Demichelis. During the game against Argentina, Chicharito was clocked running at 32.15 kilometres per hour, that's close to 20 miles per hour. That made him the fastest player in South Africa.

All this was scant consolation as Mexico were eliminated in the most disappointing circumstances. They were rightly infuriated, but their football had impressed and Chicharito could take a lot of positives from his first World Cup finals. United fans had seen enough of their new striker at the highest level to feel optimistic about the season ahead. Meanwhile the new recruit would take a well-earned rest. 2010 was set to continue to be a momentous year for Chicharito.

UNITED

united

Houston, Texas, July 2010. Manchester United are in America's biggest oil town to play the fourth game of a North American tour after matches in Toronto, Philadelphia and Kansas. The United players enjoy a day at the NASA space centre before returning to the team hotel to be introduced to a young man in jeans and a green T-shirt. His name is Javier Hernández. Sir Alex Ferguson puts a paternal arm across the Mexican's shoulders and introduces him to some of the biggest names in football. Hernández trains with the team for the first time the next day.

'I was very nervous in that first training session in Houston,' he later said. 'I was nervous because I wanted to succeed for this team. But I remember that first day in training and I enjoyed it a lot.'

Like United's other players who had played in South Africa in the World Cup finals, Hernández had been given extra time off, but he couldn't wait to get started at his new club. The feeling was mutual and the fans were anxious to see him in action.

He'd not even played a game for United, yet the name of Chicharito was on the fans' lips more than any other player. He was already a star among Houston's huge Mexican community, many of whom had seen him play in the giant Reliant Stadium for his country a few months earlier.

Despite the sweltering heat outside the stadium, hundreds gathered hours before the match in the vast car parks which surround the indoor, six-tier, 71,500 home of the Houston Texans NFL team.

Most of the noisy fans in the car park were supporters of Houston Dynamo, the local Major League Soccer side who are part-owned by the retired boxer Oscar De La Hoya.

Following a surprise defeat in Kansas City, United needed a lift in a game against the best of America's MLS league – the MLS All-Stars match. The Reds started well with Federico Macheda scoring twice in the first 11 minutes. Had you asked any United fan there that night, they would have ranked Macheda ahead of Hernández in the strikers' pecking order at Old Trafford.

An astonishing crowd of 70,728, by far the biggest of the tour, watched United outclass the hosts as the Reds concluded the American part of their three-country pre-season tour. The biggest roar of the night was not for Macheda's goals, though, but the appearance of Hernández, who came on as a 62nd-minute substitute for Nani and received a huge cheer from the thousands of Mexicans in the crowd. Hernández had been on the pitch 22 minutes when he scored his first United goal after running on to a long Paul Scholes pass before lobbing over goalkeeper Nick Rimando from 20 yards to complete an emphatic 5–2 win for United. It was the goal most of the stadium had been waiting for and Hernández didn't stop smiling for days. He smiled at all the fans as he left the pitch and at all the journalists in the mixed zone deep inside the stadium. Here was a man living the dream.

And he smiled again as the United plane flew straight from Houston and three hours south to his home city of Guadalajara. United were going to Mexico for the first time to play in a game organised to open the new Chivas stadium as part of Chicharito's transfer deal.

Hundreds of fans were waiting for United at the airport, thousands were waiting for Chicharito. United's players had become used to welcomes around the globe which resembled Beatlemania. They hadn't been accustomed to one player getting almost all the attention. Even David Beckham in his prime didn't attract so much adulation.

The Chivas board were celebrating too. Their new superb Estadio Omnilife had been the subject of ridicule in Mexico after its construction fell behind schedule: now they were bringing Manchester United's first team to town to open it.

'In our country Manchester United are thought of as the top team and the reception they will get will be fabulous,' predicted Hernández. It was.

Hernández would play one half each for his former club and his current club. He started out in a Chivas shirt and, fittingly, he became the first player to score in the new stadium after hitting a left-foot shot past Edwin van der Sar. Chris Smalling, United's other summer signing of 2010, equalised but Chivas were leading 2–1 at half-time when Chicharito swapped sides.

He replaced Dimitar Berbatov and played for United for 15 minutes. Chivas won the game, but the result of the friendly wasn't the important thing.

'Chicharito was first class,' said Sir Alex Ferguson after the game. 'His goal for Chivas was a marvellous strike. He showed his real qualities.

'It was always my intention to give him only 15 minutes of the second half as he is in the process of recovering from the World Cup. He will now do some fitness training and endurance work when he arrives in Manchester and he will play more games.'

The United manager had been impressed with Hernández's first week of training.

'Chicharito has done really well,' he said. 'The players have all remarked how good he is and what a great finisher he is – I think there are similarities between him and Ole Gunnar Solskjaer.

'The players are all supportive of him and have welcomed him to the club. I think he has a great future with us.'

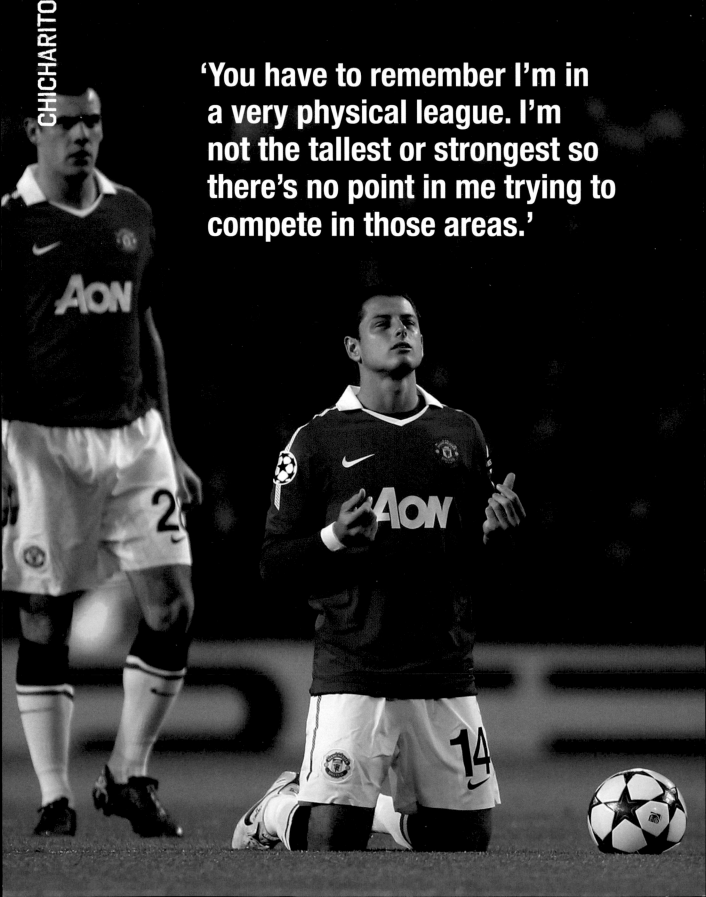

CHICHARITO

'You have to remember I'm in a very physical league. I'm not the tallest or strongest so there's no point in me trying to compete in those areas.'

As for Hernández's role in the team, Ferguson said: 'The 4–3–3 formation suits us in some games, particularly in Europe because it's important to guard against the counter-attack and keep possession.

'I think Chicharito can play as a lone striker, there's no question about that. He did it in the World Cup for Mexico. But there are big possibilities of a partnership with Wayne Rooney and other players.'

Similarities with Solskjaer? A partnership with Rooney? Such talk could only whet the appetite of every United fan ahead of the 2010–11 season.

Javier Hernández was billed as a player for the future by United. Sir Alex Ferguson didn't want him to be under too much pressure. Not every striker cuts the mustard at Old Trafford and Diego Forlán, who would be awarded the Golden Ball as the best player of the 2010 World Cup finals, struggled to score after arriving from South America in 2002. Everything else comes second to scoring when you are a striker – especially for Manchester United.

The problem was that United fans were desperate to see Hernández in that famous red shirt. They'd read about his reputation in Mexico and seen him do so well in South Africa.

Hernández moved to Manchester full-time with his family in August 2010. His mum was on hand to cook his usual food, and while he would miss out on his favourite meal of beef fillet in breadcrumbs made by his grandmother, he adopted what he called 'a positive attitude'.

'From the first day I arrived in Manchester I was determined it would be a completely positive experience,' he said. 'That's not to say that I wouldn't miss Mexico, but I wanted to look upon Manchester as my second home.'

His team-mates were impressed by his professionalism and shooting in training. In return, he described the training centre at Carrington as 'perfect'.

'The coaches have helped me with every aspect of my game and the facilities are excellent,' he explained. 'Whatever the players need the staff will help. Nothing is too much trouble.'

Chicharito didn't start in the team which faced Chelsea in the 2010 Community Shield at Wembley, as Michael Owen began up front with Wayne Rooney, but the Mexican made his English debut when he came on after half-time and converted a ball from Antonio Valencia after 75 minutes. It was a bizarre first goal in England for it misconnected with his foot and deflected off his head into the goal. If it hadn't hit his head it would have gone over the bar.

'It was an unusual goal,' he said. 'I tried to kick the ball and it went into my face.'

It was the mark of a natural goal-scorer as United won 3–1, but what was more interesting was the instant understanding between Hernández and Dimitar Berbatov.

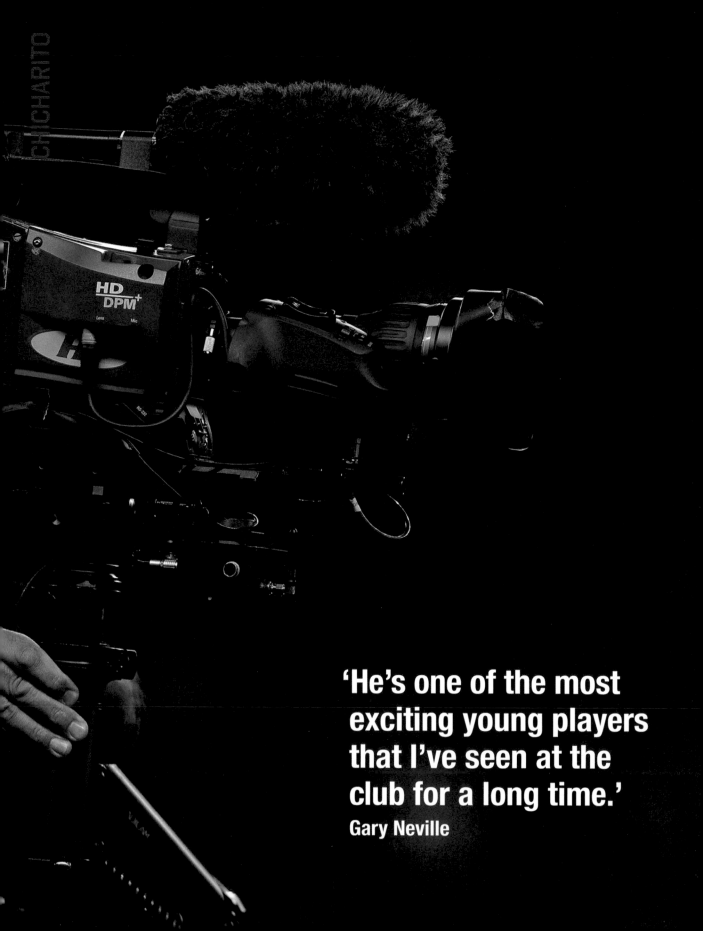

'He's one of the most exciting young players that I've seen at the club for a long time.'
Gary Neville

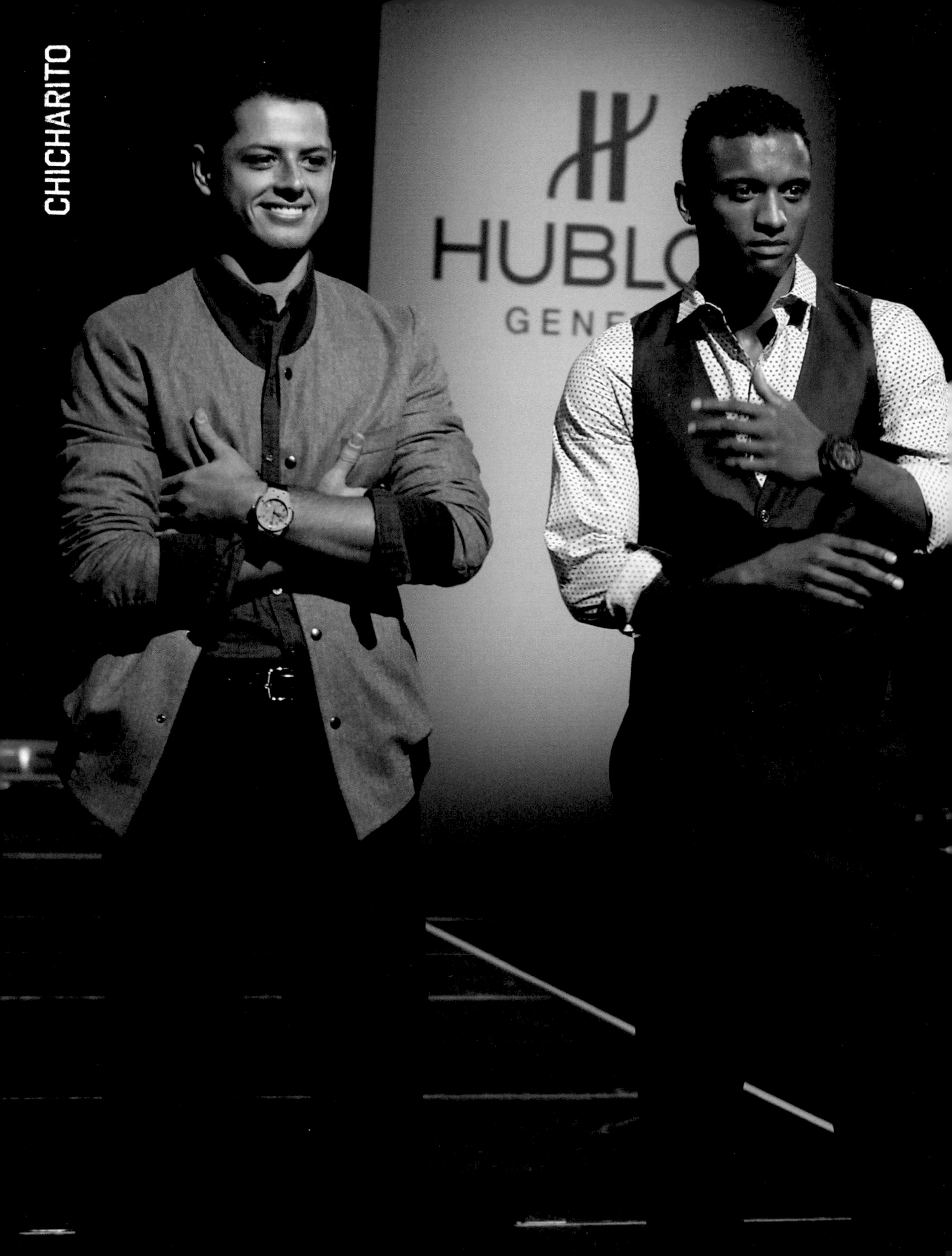

'Javier Hernández came on at half-time and fired the imagination with his eager running and clever flicks,' reported the *Guardian* newspaper. 'The young Mexican is infectiously exciting. His buzzing presence altered the tone of the game. Although he miscued when Dimitar Berbatov presented him with a chance, something told you Chicharito – "little pea" – would soon be in the groove. A few minutes later he kicked Antonio Valencia's cross against his own face and the ball bounced in. When you've got it, you've got it ...'

When it was pointed out to him later in the season that he seemed to be able to score with any part of his body, Chicharito replied, 'I've been a little lucky with some goals, but I'm just happy that they have gone in.'

Hernández left London for Mexico City and an international friendly game against recently crowned world champions Spain. It was Spain's first game since the World Cup final, the match staged to celebrate 200 years of Mexican independence ... from Spain.

Spain fielded a full side, whereas Chicharito only played the first half, but that was enough for him to give Mexico the lead in the 12th minute as he converted a cross from Guardado. And despite just playing 45 minutes, Hernández was named man of the match in all the leading Mexican newspapers. David Silva got a 90th-minute equaliser to prevent a famous victory for El Tri.

Hernández returned to Manchester where he was on the bench for United's opening league game of the 2010–11 season at home to Newcastle United. There was concern about another striker, Wayne Rooney, who had failed to score for United and England in over a thousand minutes of football, while Michael Owen's future role became clearer as he was left out of the squad.

Rooney linked up with Dimitar Berbatov but the partnership didn't impress, despite United winning 3–0. Rooney was removed, allowing the Hernández–Berbatov pairing to flourish again, and the Mexican was given a hero's reception in the 62nd minute when he took to the Old Trafford field for the first time.

Hernández made his first United Premier League start at Fulham away on 22 August. He didn't score in the 2–2 draw at Craven Cottage and was back on the bench for the next game at home to West Ham, with his grandfather keen to point out in interviews that Hugo Sánchez, arguably the greatest ever Mexican striker, 'had not conquered Europe in his first season'.

Chicharito got his first experience of Champions League football when he started against Scottish champions Rangers in a group game at Old Trafford on 14 September. Underdogs Rangers took an ultra-defensive approach to somehow shut out Chicharito and United for 90 minutes in a 0–0 draw. He didn't feature in the next match either as a Berbatov hat-trick helped beat Liverpool 3–2, but he was in

the starting line-up at Scunthorpe a few days later in the Carling Cup (where fringe players are often fielded) and again he didn't trouble the scoresheet.

Very early days still, but Hernández wasn't setting Old Trafford alight, boasting just one goal in the Community Shield. His pre-season form had raised expectations, but these were now slowly deflating.

The new signing was absent against Bolton in United's next Premier League match but came on against Valencia in a key Champions League game at the Mestalla on 29 September 2010.

Valencia were the Primera Liga leaders and in form. They worked United hard and looked the more likely side to score, with striker Roberto Soldado and winger Pablo Hernández the best performers. Chicharito was brought on as a substitute for Anderson in the 77th minute. Six minutes later he met Nani's ball and his shot rocketed on to the crossbar. Then Federico Macheda replaced Berbatov in the 85th minute. The young Italian fed a ball to Chicharito on the edge of the box; he took a superb first touch to steady himself before lashing the ball with his left foot across keeper César Sánchez and into the bottom corner. The home fans were silenced as the Mexican's devastating Solskjaer-like substitution completed a perfect European away performance.

Talk among the 2,000 travelling United fans that night in Spain's third biggest city was that the team might be on to something big with Hernández. His team-mates agreed.

'We defended as a team and got a goal on the counter-attack,' said Rio Ferdinand. 'Chicha came on and proved his worth.'

'I'm very happy for the goal,' smiled Hernández, 'but I'm even happier about the result. The Champions League is the most important tournament in the world and it's great to score my first goal in it. We also kept a clean sheet and we're top of the group. I'm happy.'

Back on the bench for United's next game, a 0–0 draw at Sunderland, Chicha started against West Brom at Old Trafford on 16 October and showed that he was finding his rhythm by scoring his third United goal after following up a Nani free-kick to put the ball in from six yards out.

October 2010 would be a month where he started one week and was named as a sub a week later. He was a substitute against Turkish champions Bursaspor at Old Trafford, but he made his best impact to date in the following away game at Stoke City.

United had drawn all four of their away league games so far, not the form of a team who wanted to win the Premier

League, especially with Chelsea racking up victories. In a tumultuous week at Old Trafford, Wayne Rooney had asked for a transfer, citing United's lack of ambition in attracting the world's top players, before changing his mind.

Rooney would watch the Stoke game from a sunlounger in Dubai, while some even pointed to Hernández as an example of those cut-price United signings rather than A-listers that Rooney was hinting at.

Chicha made them eat their words in the match at Stoke, scoring both the goals in a 2–1 win, United's first victory away in the league that season. The manner of both goals was dramatic. In the 27th minute, Nemanja Vidić headed a Nani cross across the goal. Facing away from goal, the Mexican rose and twisted his body before outrageously flicking the ball with the back of his head into the net. A brilliant, unconventional goal, fashioned from almost nothing. He ran away and celebrated by holding the United badge on his shirt up to the Stoke supporters, who are far from fond of Manchester United.

Stoke are formidable at home and equalised in the 82nd minute. United were heading for a fifth successive away draw … until Hernández got a dramatic 87th-minute winner after instinctively poking home a cross from Patrice Evra from five yards out, right in front of the 3,000 travelling Reds. The celebrations were the best of the season so far and the ecstatic fans spilled on to the pitch. And, just as with Valencia a month earlier, Stoke were too stunned to hit back.

Hernández had won a vital game for United and became a hero that afternoon.

'Javier deserved the goals because he's worked so hard since coming to the club,' said Gary Neville.

'He's tough – having grown up in Mexico,' added Neville, 'but what sets him apart for me is his work rate every single day. He's got talent and the right attributes, you obviously have to have talent to come to this club, but his work rate is phenomenal and he's one of the most exciting young players that I've seen at the club for a long time.'

Hernández was delighted but, with typical modesty, deflected the praise towards his team-mates. Asked if his first goal was lucky, he said: 'Of course, but I tried to head it in. I am enjoying my time in England. I am here to learn, to work hard and do my best for Manchester United.'

'The players are all supportive of him and have welcomed him to the club. I think he has a great future with us.'
Sir Alex Ferguson

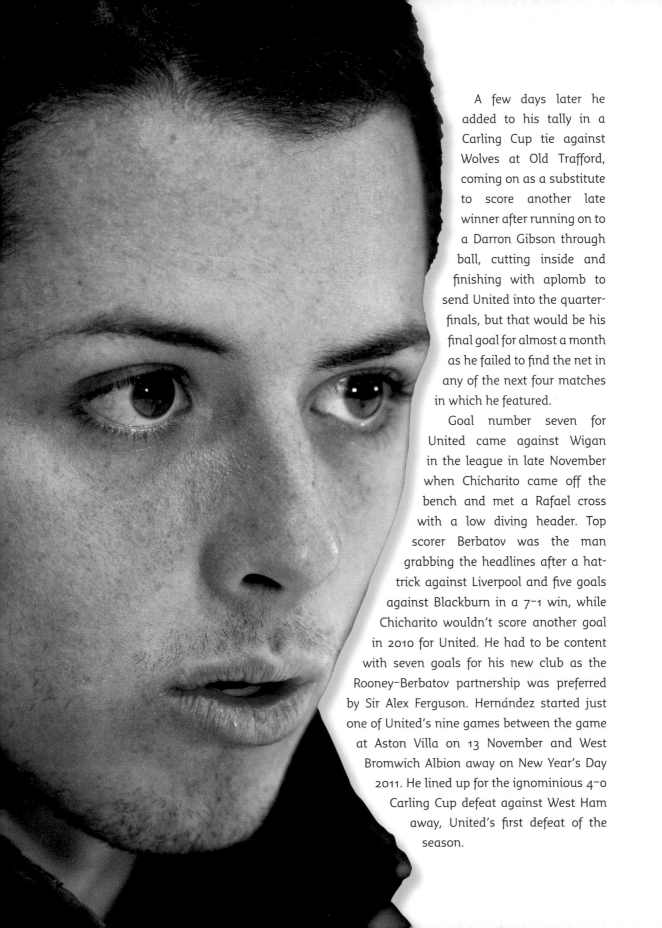

A few days later he added to his tally in a Carling Cup tie against Wolves at Old Trafford, coming on as a substitute to score another late winner after running on to a Darron Gibson through ball, cutting inside and finishing with aplomb to send United into the quarter-finals, but that would be his final goal for almost a month as he failed to find the net in any of the next four matches in which he featured.

Goal number seven for United came against Wigan in the league in late November when Chicharito came off the bench and met a Rafael cross with a low diving header. Top scorer Berbatov was the man grabbing the headlines after a hat-trick against Liverpool and five goals against Blackburn in a 7–1 win, while Chicharito wouldn't score another goal in 2010 for United. He had to be content with seven goals for his new club as the Rooney–Berbatov partnership was preferred by Sir Alex Ferguson. Hernández started just one of United's nine games between the game at Aston Villa on 13 November and West Bromwich Albion away on New Year's Day 2011. He lined up for the ignominious 4–0 Carling Cup defeat against West Ham away, United's first defeat of the season.

The West Brom game was important though. It was Gary Neville's final ever game for United and United's opening goal from Rooney was his first from open play since the previous March, but Hernández was the one who dominated the next day's papers.

United had been poor and disjointed when the Mexican, who had just spent his first Christmas outside his homeland, replaced Berbatov after 60 minutes.

With the score at 1–1 with 15 minutes to play, Chicharito peeled away from the goalkeeper to head in a corner from Rooney at the near post. The goal gave United an undeserved victory. 'Chicha comes on for us and gets himself in good positions all the time,' said Rio Ferdinand, 'and that's what he's done today.'

Rooney and Chicharito? That would become a key partnership in United's charge to a 19th league title – one that looked unlikely as United, formidable at home, stuttered in away matches. The victory at the Hawthorns was only United's second away win of the season. Chicharito had been responsible for dramatic, vital late winners in both.

The goal earned Hernández a start in United's next game at home to Stoke – the team he'd been so deadly against a few months earlier. The situation in the league had shifted in misfiring United's favour from the autumn, as the previously free-scoring leaders Chelsea suffered an alarming dip in form.

Hernández gave United the lead with a brilliant back-heel under tight pressure from the Stoke defenders after 27 minutes. Berbatov sent Nani away on the right and the Portuguese winger, who was one of United's best players of the season, hit a low cross into the edge of the six-yard box which the Mexican cheekily flicked between his legs into the corner of the net. United fans compared the strike to a great goal scored by Lee Sharpe against Barcelona in 1994.

'Hernández crafted a yard to find Nani on the edge of the box and he turned inside on to his left foot, hitting a rocket of a shot that flew past Asmir Begović's despairing dive,' raved the BBC.

'[United] are blessed with players who can make extraordinary things happen even on ordinary nights,' wrote the *Guardian*. 'Both their goals were exceptional, in very different ways – Hernández's for its ingenuity from close range and Nani's for the expertise of his long-range shot.

'Hernández's was a particular gem, an audacious finish off his heel for another classy addition to the portfolio of his first season in English football.

'Hernández is not the first player to score with this kind of flick but it is still a rarity and, for that, he deserves all the accolades that will come his way.'

Chicha's tally was now nine goals, six more than Rooney, despite being in and out of the first team.

The win saw United go three points clear at the top of the league over Manchester City, with fans beginning to believe that, with Hernández finding his scoring boots, a record 19th league title was in United's grasp, as reigning champions Chelsea were now nine points behind. United were unbeaten in 20 league matches of the season so far.

Hernández kept his place for the FA Cup 3rd-round match against Liverpool, where club legend Kenny Dalglish had just been given the manager's job for a second time, at Old Trafford a few days later. United had been knocked out by third-tier Leeds United at the same stage in the previous season. Going out to another deadly rival at home in the early stages for a second season in succession was unthinkable. Thankfully, a controversial Ryan Giggs penalty in the second minute was the difference between the two sides.

Chicharito wasn't selected to start for any of United's next three games, but he scored a crucial goal at Blackpool after replacing Rooney after 66 minutes when United were two goals down after a shambolic first half.

Hernández's impact was almost immediate as he played a part in United scoring two goals in three minutes to draw level. One on one with goalkeeper Kingson within five minutes, the Blackpool stopper did well to block the effort.

Berbatov volleyed the first before Chicharito sprang the offside trap and raced on to a Giggs pass, clinically steering the ball past Kingson from 18 yards to equalise. Another Berbatov goal gave United another late, great win as the Reds stayed top of the table. When United needed a cutting edge, the young Mexican had provided it for his 10th goal of the season. Asked if his movement inside the area came naturally, Chicharito replied: 'I think it's from watching so much football. I love the game. If

there's a match on TV then I'll watch it. I don't care who's playing, I don't care which league it is. Instead of watching films in my free time I'll sit in front of a match. And when I watch I analyse other players and am thinking about my own game. You have to remember I'm in a very physical league. I'm not the tallest or strongest so there's no point in me trying to compete in those areas. I need to use other skills or talents to get the better of defenders.'

His 11th strike was his first in the FA Cup. Alongside him up front was another new strike partner, this time Michael Owen.

United's opponents Southampton belied their status as a third-level club as they led a below-par United 1–0 at half-time. Owen got the equaliser in the

65th minute before Hernández settled the tie with another cool finish from another Giggs through ball. The link between the Welsh veteran and the Mexican striker was proving particularly fruitful for United in late January as the Mexican slid the shot home from eight yards. Another game, another match-winning goal for Chicharito.

It was back on the bench for the next three games. The season was two-thirds of the way through and the Little Pea had started just seven of United's 26 league games, well behind Rooney and Berbatov. His status as a fringe striker would shift over the next few months, but there were some moments along the way where his position at United was still unclear.

Chicharito did begin in the FA Cup 5th round at home to non-league Crawley Town, but United's performance was one to forget as the side crawled through 1–0. His next game was at Wigan on 26 February. The match came three days after a tiring trip to Marseille, which meant that Berbatov was rested and Chicha and Rooney were paired up front at the DW Stadium. Maybe Ferguson had his eye on a vital league game at Chelsea three days later. This was when United's squad rotation would really be tested and Chicharito was still a squad player rather than an automatic pick like Rooney, Nemanja Vidić or Patrice Evra.

United won 4–0, which was no surprise. The Reds had met Wigan 13 times since 2005 and won every single time, yet the scoreline was misleading, for Wigan created several chances which they didn't convert. Chicharito was on song again, scoring United's opening two goals, the first after 17 minutes when he ran towards the front post to meet a low Nani cross. He read the ball perfectly and nipped in front of Ali Al-Habsi to poke the ball past the goalkeeper from a tight angle.

'It was a terrific finish, but that's what he's good at,' said his manager Ferguson. 'His percentage (at converting chances) is very high.'

It was also a retort to those who claimed that he didn't look as dangerous when he started matches, a charge which was always levelled at Solskjaer, who was at his best later in games when the opposition defenders tired.

A one-two with Rooney led to Chicharito's second in the 74th minute.

Knocking a long clearance into Rooney's path, he cleverly stayed onside to accept a brilliant through ball in return. He had the time and composure to pick his spot from 16 yards out and slide a shot past Al-Habsi.

THE TURNING POINT

the turning point

Hernández had justified his start and maybe the manager saw something different in how he combined with Rooney that day. Strike partnerships can click at different points. Andy Cole and Dwight Yorke, the duo who would lead United towards the Treble in 1999, did just that one afternoon at Southampton. For Rooney and Hernández, the moment happened at Wigan.

The proof that Ferguson believed they had gelled as a partnership came three days later when United's team sheet was revealed an hour before a crucial league match at Stamford Bridge: Rooney and Hernández would start up front together, with top scorer Berbatov on the bench.

United lost 2–1, with Rooney getting the goal, and Ferguson reverted to the Bulgarian-Liverpudlian partnership for the following match against Liverpool at Anfield. It didn't work. United didn't turn up and were humiliatingly well beaten 3–1 by their Scouse rivals to leave them only three points ahead of Arsenal, who had a game in hand.

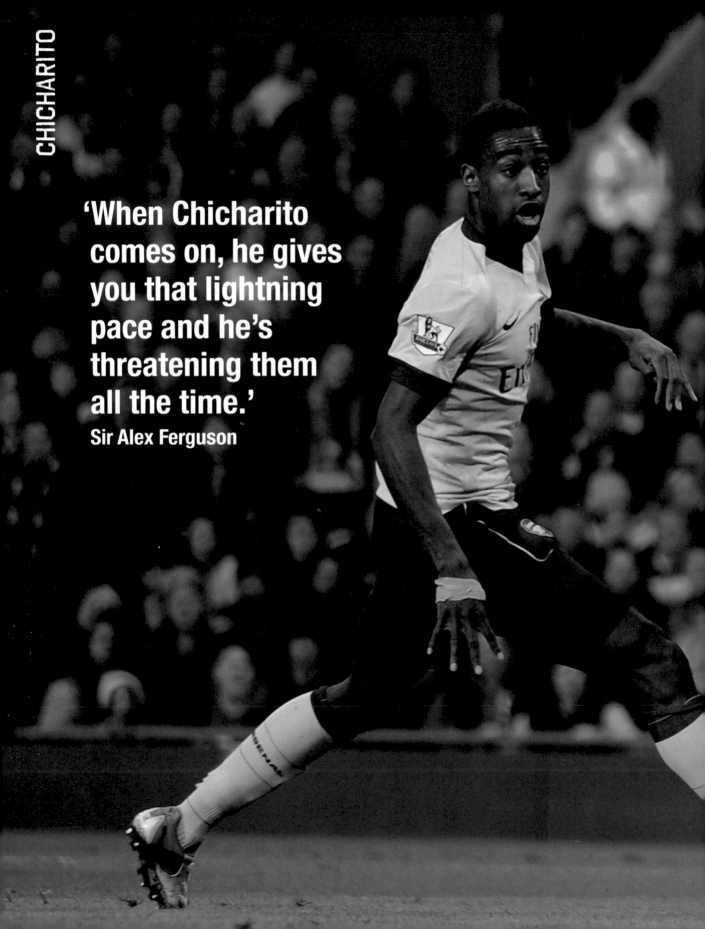

'When Chicharito comes on, he gives you that lightning pace and he's threatening them all the time.'
Sir Alex Ferguson

The big games were coming thick and fast in March 2010, the period which Fergie memorably calls 'squeaky bum time'. Hernández started the next match against Arsenal at Old Trafford in the FA Cup 6th round. United won 2–0, and although Chicharito didn't score he played a crucial role in both goals, with Fabio and Rooney both profiting from rebounds from the young Mexican's efforts. The partnership was retained for the first time as United met Marseille at home in the second leg of the Champions League last 16. This was another key turning point in his United career.

Having drawn 0–0 in the south of France, the tie was delicately poised at Old Trafford. It was a huge call by Ferguson to put his faith in the Mexican rather than the far more experienced Berbatov, who was one of the leading scorers in the Premier League. Ferguson considered the Mexican a better foil for Rooney and Chicharito would have his most important game to date, scoring twice with goals in the 5th and 75th minutes to help a nervy United overcome the French champions. Ferguson had made the right call.

Hernández showed his versatility by tapping in a Rooney cross for the first and sweeping home a low Ryan Giggs cross from close range for the second after eluding his marker. The papers were beginning to sit up and take notice, suspecting that once again Ferguson had unearthed a diamond.

'The carrot was a place in the Champions League quarter-finals and The Little Pea delivered,' said the *Sun*. 'Javier Hernández is proving to be the bargain of the season. His double took his tally for the campaign to 16 as United scrambled past Marseille.'

'Only time will tell how Hernández develops but the omens are promising,' wrote the *Daily Telegraph*. 'He has a knack of losing markers to find scoring positions that Gary Lineker would admire. He has a willingness to hound defenders in possession that echoes Ian Rush. He's a finisher who works for the team and Ferguson has bought an absolute star-in-the-making for £7 million. With Rooney dropping into the hole, Hernández led the line.'

The United manager wasn't slow to praise his two-goal hero after the game.

'When we bought him we thought that he would take some time to adjust at the club and that his main role would be as a substitute. The times he came on he won a few games for us, but now he's adjusted to the physical part of the game very well and he's adapted very well. That has given us great options. With Hernández's form the way it is, we can make some changes now.'

In Fergie-speak, that meant he felt comfortable starting him in his strongest XI. Seven months into the season and Ferguson

had found his magic combination – even if it came at the cost of leaving his top scorer out.

Rooney and Hernández would start for a third consecutive game against Bolton in the league, but it was substitute Berbatov, who replaced Hernández at half-time, who got a crucial winning goal. Having lost their two previous Premier League games, United needed the win to stay at the top of the table. The Bulgarian wasn't quite yesterday's man and it showed why United use four or five strikers in a season and don't rely on two.

Rooney demonstrated why he is United's main man in the next game as the Reds came from behind to beat West Ham 4–2 at Upton Park. Rooney got a hat-trick – and a ban for swearing at the TV cameras – but the introduction of Hernández at half-time turned around a match which had been a nightmare for United, despite the fact that the team weren't playing all that badly.

United were trailing 2–0 when Ferguson was forced to throw caution to the wind, bringing on Hernández for Evra and then Berbatov for Park Ji-Sung in the 64th minute.

'He is completely different. You can't compare him to anybody else. What has impressed me most about him, and this is something I have noticed from the first day I met him, is that he is a very simple person.'

Chicharito on Sir Alex Ferguson

Hernández got United's fourth in six minutes from a familiar source – a Giggs cross which he then poked in.

'They probably only had two shots at goal, but two-nothing down at half-time you're under the cosh,' said a relieved Ferguson after. 'I felt we had to go for it. I brought on Chicharito, put Ryan back to left-back. At that point I'm saying to myself goal difference doesn't matter. Let's get something out of it.

'When Chicharito comes on, he gives you that lightning pace and he's threatening them all the time behind. So it meant they were going right back towards the box and gave us a lot of space to operate.'

The record 19th title which seemed dead at half-time appeared very much on after 90 minutes.

United now faced Chelsea away in the Champions League quarter-final first leg. It was the biggest game of the season so far and United's poor record at Stamford Bridge didn't inspire the travelling fans.

As a measure of how his stature had grown and how he had exceeded all expectations, Hernández started up front with Rooney. United showed their ability to turn it on in big games and were excellent, with the Mexican working tirelessly to close down the Chelsea players. Rooney grabbed a vital away goal to put United a touch closer to the semi-finals, but Hernández could be delighted with his performance. He was rested and didn't get off the bench in the next Premier League game at home to Fulham, but started

'When it comes time for me to retire, I will be proud to say I was one of Sir Alex's players.'

against Chelsea in the second leg. Chicharito was now being saved for the biggest matches and with good reason. He didn't disappoint, netting the game's opening goal in the 43rd minute to almost put the tie beyond Chelsea. The goal came after John O'Shea found an opening with a ball to Giggs, who crossed to Hernández, who in turn inelegantly bundled the ball into the roof of the net with his striker's instinct to score in whatever way he can. Cue bedlam at Old Trafford as a trip to Germany to play Schalke 04 beckoned.

'Hernández was full of movement and menace,' wrote the BBC, 'in sharp contrast to Torres, who played in a fog of lost confidence.'

'Little Pea, little fee,' purred the *Guardian* as they praised his play. 'In terms of value for money, Hernández already looks assured of joining Peter Schmeichel, Eric Cantona, Ole Gunnar Solskjaer et al as one of the best signings Ferguson has ever made.'

Chicharito was asked about his relationship with his boss.

'He is completely different,' he said. 'You can't compare him to anybody else. What has impressed me most about him, and this is something I have noticed from the first day I met him, is that he is a very simple person.

'You can talk about all the things he has won and all the years he's been in charge but you wouldn't know it if you watched him on the bench. Every game looks like it is his first. He is so excited. So enthusiastic. He wants to win so much. That is the key. He will never get bored of winning and he enjoys what he does.

'Not only that, Ferguson never forgets that his players are all humans, rather than simple cogs to fit into machines. Every day he will ask me how I am feeling, whether I am OK and whether I need anything. He is just an unbelievable person. He recognises that first you are a human being and then you are a football player.'

This was one very happy player speaking as he added: 'Manchester United is the best club in the world so you would always want to come here, but to be part of one of Sir Alex's teams was a huge factor. I hope he stays on for a few more years and then, when it comes time for me to retire, I will be proud to say I was one of Sir Alex's players.'

United couldn't relax for one minute. An improving Manchester City were the next opponents in the FA Cup semi-final at Wembley. Hernández didn't start, but two missed chances from Berbatov would count in his favour. Could the Bulgarian be trusted in those absolutely vital matches where United might only get one half-chance? That's what fans asked as they skulked out of Wembley having seen City win 1–0. There would be no Treble in 2010–11.

Their mood would be lifted as Hernández got his 19th goal of the season in dramatic circumstances against Everton on 23 April 2011. With Chicha starting up front alongside Rooney, United were nervy against an in-form Everton who'd held the Reds at Goodison earlier in the season. United needed a win, but appeared to be heading for an unwanted draw when Hernández saw a header brilliantly tipped over by Tim Howard nine minutes from time. The clock was ticking down, but the Mexican only needs a second to score a goal. And his contribution in the 84th minute would be crucial – a brave header at the far post from a cross by Antonio Valencia. Hernández's reactions were incredible to pick up the cross, which deflected off Sylvain Distin. United were nine points clear of title rivals Arsenal and Chelsea and the proud son of Guadalajara was again the reason why.

He gave an interview after the game where he described the match as a 'wonderful result'.

'We need to think game by game,' he added with a note of caution.

Chicha also translated for Anderson, whose grasp of English was still suspect after three years in Manchester. It was a comedy moment as the question was asked

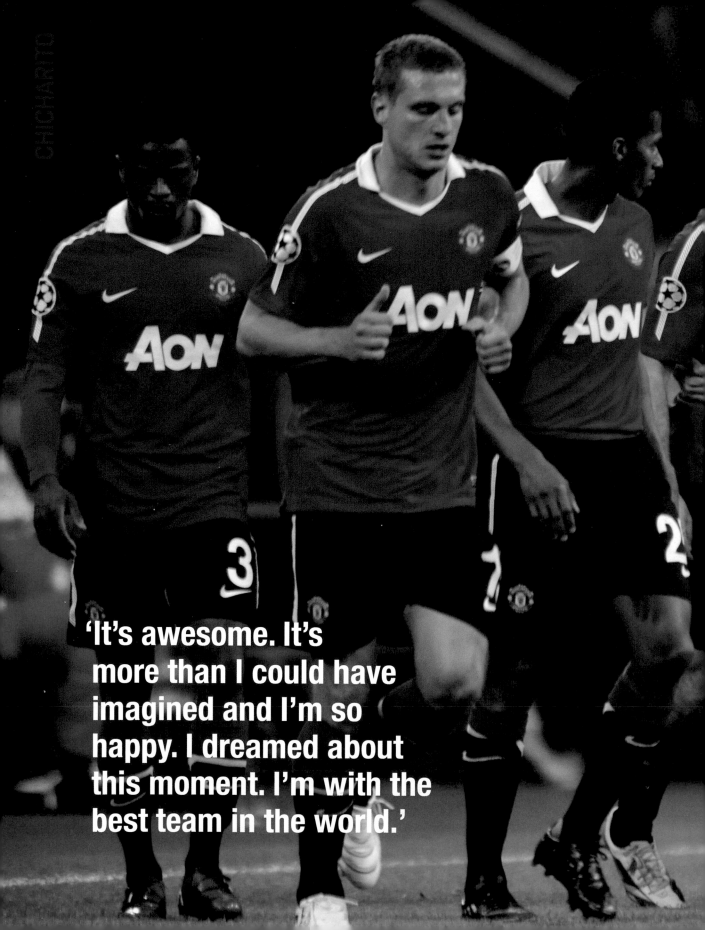

'It's awesome. It's more than I could have imagined and I'm so happy. I dreamed about this moment. I'm with the best team in the world.'

in English, which Hernández translated into Spanish. Anderson replied in Portuguese and Hernández reported his answer back in English.

'The boy is a natural goal-scorer,' added Ferguson. 'He's tremendously quick with two good feet. He's very good in the air.'

Hernández and Rooney would link up again against Schalke 04 in the Champions League semi-final first leg in Germany. Asked about Hernández, Rooney said, 'He's just taken everything in his stride. He's a lovely lad, who's always smiling around the dressing room, and on the pitch he's been brilliant. You can see he's got a natural eye for goal, but what surprised a lot of us is how good he is in the air. He spends ages practising after training and he's been a great asset for us this season.'

It may have been the semi-final of the biggest club tournament in the world, but United completely dominated the German side and won 2–0, with Hernández setting up Rooney for the second goal. The Reds were now named odds-on favourites to reach a third Champions League final in four years against Barcelona or Real Madrid, who were literally battling their matches out over 180 minutes in Spain.

United dropped league points against Arsenal days later after suffering another Euro hangover, then duly beat Schalke 04 easily 4–1 at Old Trafford, a game Chicharito was rested for. Had United not enjoyed a two goal cushion from the away leg, Hernández would surely have started. Now he was first choice, he had to be rested where appropriate as there were no easy games ahead. League challengers Chelsea believed they could do serious damage to United's season at Old Trafford. Chelsea captain John Terry claimed that his in-form side, who had enjoyed a late surge, could beat United at Trafford and snatch the title.

It was wishful thinking. The beautiful and balanced Rooney–Hernández partnership would lead the line. United went in front after just 36 seconds when Chicharito received a pass from Park.

'This was United at their best, moving with speed and skill, giving an opponent little chance to form a meaningful barricade,' wrote the *Daily Telegraph*. 'Giggs teased a pass to Park, who let the ball run across him and then swept it forward. Chelsea had a split second to stifle the whirlwind, to keep their title dream alive. They missed it. David Luiz should have cut Park's ball out. He missed.

'Hernández did not. A twitch of the Mexican's shoulders wrong-footed Petr Čech, a strike from his right boot sent the ball racing into the net, bringing almost a guttural roar from the United support.'

It was the furthest from the net that the Mexican had been for any of his 20 goals. United won 2–1. The title was within touching distance as the team just needed one point with two games to play. They were now within touching distance of a record-breaking 19th league title – and fulfilling Alex Ferguson's ambition to 'knock

Liverpool off their perch'. When Ferguson took charge of United in November 1986, United had just seven league titles to Liverpool's 16. Liverpool won two more before United's dominance of English football began in 1993.

The Premier League was won at Ewood Park a week later when Hernández again started with Rooney. The Reds agonisingly went a goal down and were still trailing in the 70th minute when Paul Robinson rashly brought down Chicharito to concede a penalty. Maybe United were fortunate because, while Robinson had made contact with the striker, United's number 14 had knocked the ball forward and had little chance of reaching it. Blackburn's manager Steve Kean felt that Hernández 'was going down before the goalkeeper caught him'. None of this mattered; Rooney converted the penalty and United were champions.

The players celebrated on the pitch in front of the 7,000 United fans – many of them wearing Mexican sombreros in tribute – celebrating in the Darwen End.

Interviewed on the pitch by the Sky TV cameras, Chicharito said, 'It's awesome. It's more than I could have imagined and I'm so happy. I dreamed about this moment. I'm with the best team in the world.'

He was again rested as Blackpool were beaten – and relegated – in the final league game as United's attentions turned to the Champions League final against Barcelona. United were already champions and didn't want to risk players like Chicharito if possible. In an interview the week before the final game at Wembley, Hernández again expressed his gratitude to Sir Alex Ferguson.

'He's just taken everything in his stride. He's a lovely lad, who's always smiling around the dressing room.'
Wayne Rooney

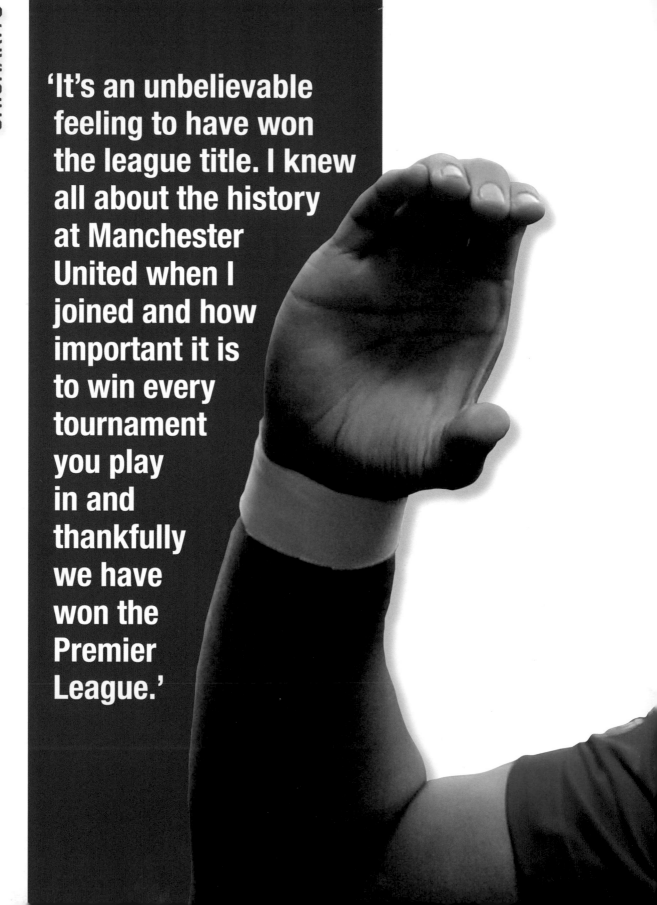

'It's an unbelievable feeling to have won the league title. I knew all about the history at Manchester United when I joined and how important it is to win every tournament you play in and thankfully we have won the Premier League.'

'The coach always looks out for me,' he explained. 'Because it's my first year away from home he checks if I'm well and happy. When there are games or training he tells me things. He says: "Move your body this way," or talks to me about movement. There's lots of advice he gives me and I try to be a sponge so I can soak up every tip.'

Asked the secret of his success, Chicharito replied: 'Working hard is the secret of success in life, not just in football but in every job. I try to work hard on my physical side too because I'm not a very strong player by nature, nor am I very tall. There have been many great players here so you always have to give something extra.

'It's easy playing here because all the other strikers are world class, not just Rooney but all of them. You can see that in the way they play but the most important thing is not individuals but the team winning.

'Football is my life and I can see that with my other team-mates. Football is our life, we love the sport very much. It's just incredible that I can finish my first season at my new club playing in the Champions League final at Wembley.'

Barcelona were the opponents in a re-run of the 2009 final which the Catalans had won so convincingly. Barça were favourites, but their star man Lionel Messi picked out Chicharito as United's danger man. The world's best player did him the honour of singling him out for praise.

Chicharito would become only the second Mexican after Rafael Márquez to play in a Champions League final. Life was wonderful, but United were outclassed again and lost 3–1 in a game that pretty much passed Hernández by. Perhaps it was one match too many for him in a hectic first season at Old Trafford. Barcelona were brilliant and justified their status as the best team in the world with a second Champions League final triumph over United in three years. United were the top dogs in England; Barcelona in Spain and the world. Chicharito was almost helpless as the best players in the business, stars like Lionel Messi, Xavi Hernández and Andres Iniesta, dominated play and almost toyed with United. Rather than become too despondent though, he found strength in the adversity.

'It was a lesson and we can learn from that,' a suited Chicharito said in the mixed zone after the match.

'We have to credit Barça as they are the best team in the world but we will move forward, that's what we have always done in the history of this club.'

Hernández had scored 20 goals in his first season in England, almost a goal every other appearance, many of which had been as a substitute. Most of his goals came in the last 15 minutes of matches and nine of the 20 were match-winning goals.

That's not all. In a season where United won a record 19th league title and reached the final of the Champions League for the third time in four years, Chicharito was the only player to score in each of the five competitions United played in. Thirteen of his goals came in the league, four in the Champions League and one apiece in the FA Cup, Carling Cup and Community Shield.

The variety of goals was pleasing too. He scored ten with his right foot, four with his left and six with his head.

Most of Chicharito's goals were not spectacular, but lethal, as he hit the ball low into either corner. His runs across the box were also deadly as he notched up several close-range efforts. Half the goals came from inside the six-yard box, half outside. Not a single one of his goals was scored from outside the penalty area. Chicharito is a pure predator, like Ruud van Nistelrooy or Gary Lineker.

His goals tally was even more impressive when you consider that he only started 15 of United's 38 league games. Ten players all started more games than the Mexican, yet such was Chicharito's influence in other competitions and from coming on as a sub, altogether he featured in 45 games for United in his first season. So much for him being one for the future, he was one for now. His 20 goals were only one behind Berbatov as United's leading scorer and he bagged four more than Rooney.

United fans honoured the Mexican by voting for him to be given the club's prestigious Sir Matt Busby Player of the Year Award. Chicharito picked up 21 per cent of the votes to pip Nani (20 per cent) into second place, with captain Nemanja Vidić (16 per cent) completing the top three. He was presented with the award by Gary Neville at a special night at Old Trafford and became the sixth player to win the award at the end of his first season, following Brian McClair in 1988, Gary Pallister in 1990, Ruud van Nistelrooy in 2002, Cristiano Ronaldo in 2004 and Gabriel Heinze in 2005.

'I have to say thank you so much to the fans,' he said. 'They have helped me a lot. I think this was a difficult decision to make and I don't think I deserve it because it hasn't been just one player who has played well. We are a team.

'I also must thank my family who came over to England with me and helped me a lot, and of course I've had great support from the boss, my team-mates, the coaches and all the staff at the club who have all helped me feel very happy and very comfortable here.

'I dreamed about playing for Manchester United and thought perhaps in my first season I'd play for the Reserves with maybe a few minutes in the first team. But thanks to the boss and all my team-mates I have played a little bit more!

'It's an unbelievable feeling to have won the league title. I knew all about the history at Manchester United when I joined and how important it is to win every tournament you play in and thankfully we have won the Premier League.'

It had been a wonderful first year for Javier 'Chicharito' Hernández and, with his sublime talent and commitment, there can only be more to come.

back to the future

Javier Hernández had no time to dwell on the mixed emotions of joy at United's 19th title win and the crushing disappointment of their Champions League defeat at Wembley. In the summer of 2011, Chicha faced the fresh challenge of the CONCACAF Gold Cup with Mexico – the regional cup for the Americas similar to the Copa America or the European Championship.

Mexicans were still digesting the success of Chicharito's brilliant first season in Manchester as they looked forward to the competition when Tomás Balcázar, Javi's grandfather, was asked about how his grandson had suddenly become the most famous current Mexican player on the planet.

'He's got a great physique and knows how to use it – what's the point in having really big, strong muscles if it makes you slower?' he said. 'He moves at the speed and with the power that is required in European leagues. I was saying to his dad that Chicharito makes some diagonal runs that I've never seen in any Mexican player. He makes diagonal runs and he's not bothered if he gets the ball or not because he leaves a team-mate free by taking the markers away.'

Asked if there were any similarities with his dad or grandad in his playing style, Tomás agreed and said: 'In heading and his big jump. His dad measures just over a metre and a half in height. With his shortness, he'd jump for a header and seem to be suspended by cable in the air.'

For the first time, Chicharito had become the key Mexican international player as the Gold Cup approached.

Mexico were one of 12 competing countries along with tournament hosts USA and teams like Honduras, Canada and Cuba. Maybe it's not at the same level as tournaments in Europe or South America, but it's taken very seriously by the

CHICHARITO

competing nations and tickets for some of America's biggest stadiums were sold out throughout the tournament.

Mexican preparations did not go well as five of their players tested positive for clenbuterol – a performance-enhancing drug. They claimed that their food had been contaminated.

When Mexico's tournament got under way on 5 June in front of 80,108 fans in the spectacular Dallas Cowboys stadium, they beat El Salvador 5–0 thanks to a sensational Hernández hat-trick in the last 30 minutes. He bagged another two in another 5–0 victory, this time over Cuba four days later, and another goal in a 2–1 quarter-final win against Guatemala in New Jersey.

The semi-finals pitted El Tri against fellow 2010 World Cup finalists Honduras in front of over 70,000 at the Reliant Stadium in Houston. Mexico ended the 0–0 stalemate of the first 90 minutes by scoring twice in extra-time, the second from Hernández in the 99th minute. Mexico were through to the final, where they would play the host nation, their old rival the United States of America, in the Rose Bowl.

A sell-out crowd of 93,420 saw Chicharito's team beat the US 4–2 and, while he wasn't on the scoresheet in the final, he finished as the tournament's top scorer with seven – three more than the second-placed player. Chicharito was also selected in the tournament's best team and won best player of the tournament as Mexico remained undefeated throughout.

United wanted Chicharito to have a good rest following the Gold Cup final on 25 June. The United team flew to America two weeks later to start a five-game pre-season tour, but Chicharito was given a full month off as he basked in the glory of becoming a global football star. Despite pressure from the organisers of United's games, who naturally wanted to see the shooting star turn out, he wouldn't feature in America apart from at public appearances.

Back in Manchester, Chicharito's cherubic face appeared on a huge Nike advertising billboard which bridged the main Chester Road by Old Trafford.

The number of United shirts with his name on the back began to match those of Wayne Rooney – kids loved the Mexican and his good-natured, clean-cut image. They wanted to be like him.

In Mexico, United became the second most popular team outside the country after Barcelona, who have traditionally enjoyed a large support in a country which shares the Spanish language.

There are countless unofficial websites dedicated to Chicharito but he has refused to join Twitter. People began to call him the Mexican David Beckham, football's new poster boy. But Chicharito

'Playing for Manchester United has been a dream come true for me.'

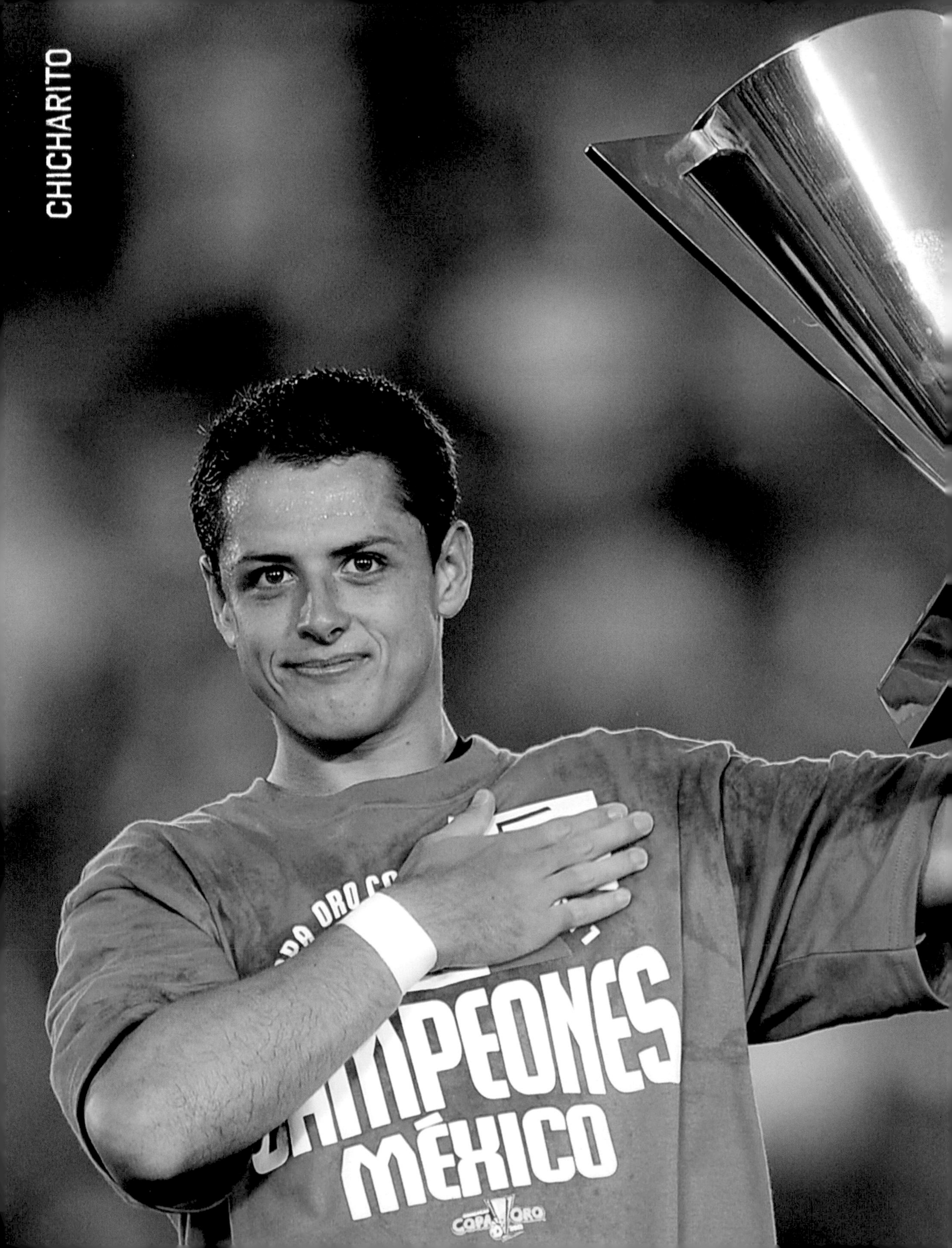
MÉXICO

doesn't court popularity, preferring to let people form their opinions of him by what they see on the football pitch and not what he says off it. His interviews are always positive and his comments can border on bland. This leaves it up to others to describe his personality, like his proud grandad, who is always his biggest supporter: 'He's a very quiet boy. He's 100 per cent professional. He doesn't drink or smoke or stay up to all hours. He won't even go out to the cinema sometimes. He prefers to come home after training, eat and then sleep.'

When United arrived in New York for the pre-season games in July 2011, Beckham was asked about Chicharito.

'I think it's great how he has adjusted to a different country and a different style of football,' said United's former number 7. 'Great players can do that. He's still a young kid but Sir Alex Ferguson has been renowned for giving kids a chance. People have been surprised at the way he's played and the goals he has scored, but he's taken his chances. He deserves everything that he's achieved.'

'My targets? To improve, keep learning and to enjoy myself.'

Despite all this acclaim, back at United, there was speculation about whether Chicharito would sign a new contract. Real Madrid were linked with him and while it was unfounded speculation, such rumours unnerve United fans after losing Cristiano Ronaldo to Madrid in 2009. It was all talk and Chicharito remained happily at United. His team-mates continued to praise him too.

'He's a lovely lad who is great for us around the dressing room,' said Rooney. 'Me and him do a lot of finishing after sessions to try and keep progressing and getting better.

'It's great to have a lad who has just come into the team, who speaks good English and is always smiling. It's great for him and for me to have someone like that.'

Talking of the possibility of Hernández suffering from the dreaded 'second-season syndrome' in English football as defenders get used to the Mexican's style of play, Rooney said: 'Of course people know about him now but, if you look at all the top players around the world, people know how they play and it's still difficult to stop them.

'I'm sure people will know a bit more about him but his movement is so good it's difficult to defend against. It won't be easy for players to defend against him whether they know about him or not.'

And praising his immediate impact, Rooney said: 'He was a young lad in his first season and I probably didn't think he was going to play as many games as he did. Once he got into the team, he took his chance and the manager kept him in. He repaid the manager with goals and was brilliant for us last season – a big reason why we won the league.

'I'm looking forward to him doing the same, if not scoring more goals for us, this season.'

Chicharito spoke of his own aims.

'My targets?' he said. 'To improve, keep learning and to enjoy myself. Hopefully in 10 years I'll still be here and saying the same thing, because this life – playing for United – is a dream for me, and I just want to keep enjoying it and working hard. The younger players run a little more and want to show why they are in the team, and that can only be good for us. But it's great because there are other players here with lots of experience too.'

Asked about the influence of his father and grandfather, he said: 'It is an advantage having them in my life and I'm following in their footsteps. They help me a lot on the pitch, as they were also attacking players, but they've helped me even more off the pitch. That's the most difficult part for young footballers – there's a lot of money and many things can put you off balance. We start very young in this profession, I'm 23 now, which is still young. I've taken a lot from both my parents, and the women in my family have helped me make sure I feel

'Some days I wake up and I just can't believe it. I'm living in this great country and playing for the best club in the world in the best league in the world. I'm so thankful for that.'

the same as other people. I'm not bigger than anybody else, despite any goals, success and medals.'

He was happy in his private life too, with long-term girlfriend Leticia 'Lety' Sahagun from Guadalajara, a beautiful and intelligent girl Chicharito knew before he became a star.

United announced the news that Hernández had signed a new five-year deal, which will see the striker stay at Old Trafford until the end of the 2015–16 season, the day after losing 6–1 at home to Manchester City in October 2011. It was a case of trying to deliver some good news on a morning when United fans were feeling very low.

On the day he signed, Sir Alex Ferguson said: 'The last player I remember making an impact as big and as quickly as Javier is Ole Gunnar Solskjaer and he reminds me of Ole a lot.

'His talent for creating space in the box and his finishing ability mark him out as a natural goal-scorer. Off the pitch, he is a pleasure to manage. He works very hard and is a popular member of the squad.'

After overcoming an injury said to be related to concussion picked up after a pre-season training session, Chicharito had started the 2011–12 season well and scored two at Bolton, a key equaliser at Anfield and a winning goal at Everton. Once he'd signed his new contract, Chicharito said: 'Playing for Manchester United has been a dream come true for me. I never expected my first year to go so well and I'm delighted to commit my future to United.

'To win a title and appear in a Champions League final was fantastic. I'm looking forward to helping my team-mates as we bid to win more trophies for this great club.

'Some days I wake up and I just can't believe it. I'm living in this great country and playing for the best club in the world in the best league in the world. I'm so thankful for that.'

So are Manchester United fans, who have seen a previously unknown signing flourish into a global superstar.

Reds have loved watching his progress and can't wait to see what the future holds, for Javier 'Chicharito' Hernández has the potential to become a United legend and Mexico's greatest footballing export since Hugo Sánchez.

acknowledgements

I would like to thank my family and friends for their support during the writing of *Chicharito*. For aiding the research of this book, I would also like to acknowledge: *Daily Telegraph*; *Diario de Guadalajara*; *Guardian*; *Independent*; *Inside United*; *Los Angeles Times*; *Manchester Evening News*; *Mural* (Guadalajara); *New York Times*; *Record* (Mexico); *Sun*; *The Times*; *The United Review*; *United We Stand*; BBC Sport; CNN (Mexico); ESPN (Mexico); MUTV; chivascampeon.com; fifa.com; informador.com.mx; manutd.com; news.bbc.co.uk/sport; soccernet. espn.go.com; uefa.com; youtube.com.